Experiencing
the Heart
of Christianity

DEDICATION

For friends in the faith community
at Penticton United Church
in their commitment
to being passionate believers today

TIM SCORER

FOREWORD BY MARCUS BORG

A 12 SESSION PROGRAM FOR GROUPS

Experiencing

The Heart
of
Christianity

WOOD LAKE BOOKS

Editor: Michael Schwartzentruber
Cover and design: Margaret Kyle
Proofreading: Dianne Greenslade

WOOD LAKE BOOKS INC. acknowledges the financial support of the Government of Canada, through the Book Publishing Industry Development Program (BPIDP) for its publishing activities.

At Wood Lake Books, we practice what we publish, being guided by a concern for fairness, justice, and equal opportunity in all of our relationships with employees and customers.

Wood Lake Books is an employee-owned company, committed to caring for the environment and all creation. Wood Lake Books recycles, reuses, and encourages readers to do the same. Resources are printed on recycled paper and more environmentally friendly groundwood papers (newsprint), whenever possible. The trees used are replaced through donations to the Scoutrees For Canada Program. A percentage of all profit is donated to charitable organizations.

Library and Archives Canada Cataloguing in Publication
A catalogue record for this publication is available from the National Library of Canada.
ISBN 1-55145-511-0

Published by WOOD LAKE BOOKS, INC.
9025 Jim Bailey Road, Kelowna, BC, Canada,
V4V 1R2
www.woodlakebooks.com
250.766.2778

Printing 10 9 8 7 6 5 4 3 2 1
Printed in Canada by
Transcontinental Printing

CREDITS

Scripture quotations are from the New Revised Standard Version of the Bible, copyright 1989 by the Division of Christian Education of the National Council of Churches of Christ in the USA. All rights reserved. Used by permission.

"Prayer of Jesus" (or "Prayer in Christ") from Jim Cotter, *Prayer at Night*, Cairns Publications, Sheffield, 1988; *Prayer at Night's Approaching*, Cairns Publications, Sheffield, 1998, and Morehouse Publishing, Harrisburg, 1998. Used by permission.

"Spirit of Life" by Carolyn McDade. Words and music by Carolyn McDade. Copyright © 1981 Carolyn McDade. Used by permission

Art work on DVD:

"Calling Disciples" by He Qi. www.heqiarts.com. (Also on cover, first image on left.) Used by permission.

"Icon of Christ" from Getty Royalty-free Images, www.gettyimages.com. (Also used on cover, second from left). Used by permission.

"The Good Shepherd." Painting by Anne C. Brink. For more information, see www.annebrink.com. (Also on cover, third from right.) Used by permission.

"Jesus" painting by Father Jerome Esser. (Also used on cover, second from right.) Every effort has been made to locate the copyright holder. Anyone with information is encouraged to contact the publisher, who will provide compensation for the use of this image upon proof of copyright ownership.

"Sanctuary" wood carving by Mary Ann Osborne, SSND. (Also used on cover far right and inset.) For further information contact 507-389-4224. Used by permission.

"One Who Broke Through the Darkness" woodcut by Mary Ann Osborne, SSND. Copyright © 1994 Mary Ann Osborne, SSND. For further information contact 507-389-4224. Used by permission.

"Yellow Christ" by Paul Gauguin, Erich Lessing, Art Resource. Used by permission.

"One," by Kristin Kennedy and Jerry Holsopple. Copyright © Jerry Holsopple and Kristin Kennedy. Used by permission.

"Jesus and the Paralysed Man" by Vie de Jesus Mafa – 24 rue Maréchal Joffre F. Versailles. www.jesusmafa.com. Used by permission.

"Baptism at Aldinga Beach" by Barbara Harris. Copyright © VISCOPY/ SODART 2001. Used by permission. (Projection permission for one week only.)

"Christ Calming the Sea" by Ignacio Fletes, *The Gospel in Art by The Peasants of Solentiname*. Used by permission.

"There came a Samaritan woman to draw water" by Olivia Silva, *The Gospel in Art by The Peasants of Solentiname*. Used by permission.

DVD production:

Video clips of Tim Scorer by Ralph Milton
Video clips of Marcus Borg by Tim Rooney, iow@imagina.com
Video editing and design by Spiro Vouladakis,
Boom Visual.Communicators, www.boomvisual.com

Table of Contents

PART TWO: SEEING THE CHRISTIAN LIFE AGAIN

FOREWORD

I am very pleased with and excited about this program based on my book *The Heart of Christianity*. I know and have worked with Tim Scorer, the author of this guide. Tim is a staff associate in ministry leadership in the United Church of Canada. I first met him when, as the program director at Naramata Centre (a retreat and educational center of the United Church of Canada, in British Columbia), he invited me to and hosted me for a couple of retreats at the Centre. He is now a member of the Ministry Leadership Team at Penticton United Church.

Tim is a superb educator. He understands both the intellectual and experiential dimensions of the Christian life extremely well. He is conceptually gifted. And he is especially gifted in small group formation and process. I am delighted to be collaborating with him in this project.

In this foreword, I want to highlight three themes that make this study guide important.

A Major Need in the Church Today

One of the most urgent needs for congregations in mainline churches in North America today is adult *re-education*. The reason: the vision of Christianity that most of us over 40 (and many under 40) learned as we were growing up in the church has ceased to be persuasive and compelling. Most of us learned a form of what I call "an earlier Christianity," a vision of the Christian life and of what it means to be Christian shaped by "an earlier Christian paradigm."

This vision has been the most common form of Christianity in Western Christianity for the past three centuries. More fully described in Chapter 1 of *The Heart of Christianity*, the earlier vision of Christianity emphasized the divine origin of the Bible as the unique revelation of God, and a literal and factual interpretation of the Bible as the story of God's acts in the past and God's requirements of belief and behavior. Its understanding of salvation emphasized the afterlife: salvation was about "going to heaven." And it affirmed that Christianity is the only true religion and thus the only way of salvation.

This is the understanding of Christianity that our parents and ancestors learned and believed. For many of them, it worked, in that it mediated a sense of the reality of God and how to live. It nourished their lives. But for millions of Christians today, its central affirmations have become difficult, even incredible.

There is more than one reason that the earlier Christian vision has become unpersuasive. One is the collision between this earlier vision and what we have learned from the study of science and history. When the Bible is interpreted literally and factually, it conflicts with much of what many of us now accept with considerable certainty.

Another reason is the moral conflict between our experience and a literal and absolutist interpretation of the Bible as the revealed will of God. Is it really true that God has commanded us not to wear garments made of two kinds of cloth (Leviticus 19:19)? Or a more timely example: many of us are now convinced that sexual orientation is either genetically given or shaped very early in life. Given this, does it make sense to see the Bible's statements about homosexuality as reflecting the absolute and eternal will of God? Does it not make more sense to see the Bible's pronouncements about this and other matters as the product of ancient communities?

A third reason is our growing awareness of religious pluralism. Many of us are struck by the saintly lives we see in other religious traditions and are unable to believe that the God of the whole universe chose to be known in only one religious tradition, which just happens to be our own.

Thus the form of Christianity that most of us learned early in our lives needs to be unlearned and replaced by a vision of Christianity that takes seriously both the Christian tradition and who we have become at the beginning of the 21st century. This is the major Christian educational task of our time.

An Emerging Christianity

We live in an exciting time in the life of the church. In the past few decades, an emerging vision of Christianity has begun to take root among both clergy and laity in mainline denominations in North America. It is a vision of Christianity that takes the Bible, God, and Jesus just as seriously as did the earlier vision of Christianity.

But the emerging vision removes the unnecessary intellectual stumbling blocks generated by the earlier vision. Rather than seeing the Bible as an inerrant or infallible divine product, it recognizes that the Bible is the product of ancient Israel and early Christianity. As such, it tells us about our spiritual ancestors' lives with God: their experiences of God, their stories about God, and what they thought life with God involved. Rather than emphasizing a literal-factual reading of the Bible, it recognizes that the Bible often uses the language of metaphor and poetry to speak about God and God's relation to the world. And rather than emphasizing what we must do or believe in order to have a blessed afterlife, the emerging Christian vision emphasizes a relationship with God in the present that transforms our lives in this life.

I suspect that this guide to *The Heart of Christianity* will be of greatest interest to mainline Christians. But what I call an emerging Christianity is developing not only in mainline denominations, but also in some parts of evangelical Christianity. There it is commonly called "emergent Christianity." For an introduction to this conversation among evangelicals, I especially recommend Brian McLaren's most recent book, *A Generous Orthodoxy*.

Though still very much a minority voice among evangelicals, its advocates cite their dismay with the rigidity of much of evangelical theology, its shallow worship (even though it may be enthusiastic), and its inadequate awareness of the rich resources of religious practices in the Christian tradition. These are also among the factors that have contributed to the development of emerging Christianity in mainline denominations, and thus I hope that this guide will also find a readership among evangelicals who have become disenchanted with some of the emphases of their communities.

Sharing the Christian Journey

Beginning a couple of decades ago, what is sometimes called "the small group movement" is making a significant impact in the life of some congregations. These small groups provide a context for Christians to share their faith journeys in a community of intimacy and companionship.

In my experience, Christians are deeply nourished by such sharing. Yet many report that their church has provided little opportunity to do so. This guide provides such an opportunity. One of its major strengths is its use of an interactive approach that integrates education about Christianity with intimate sharing of the group's lived experience, as well as worship. As I mentioned earlier, Tim Scorer is a masterful architect of group formation and group process. Participants will find themselves drawn into an exploration of their own religious and spiritual journeys in the context of re-education about what it means to be Christian.

The development of intimate communities of sharing is analogous to what we know of earliest Christianity, especially as we see it in the letters of Paul. What we somewhat misleadingly call the "churches" of Paul were small communities, perhaps as small as ten or 20 people. Their size fostered intimacy as their members learned together what it meant to follow Jesus; "to be imitators of Christ," as Paul put it. They came to know each other well and became a community of support for each other, even as they also became an "alternative community," a group of people living with a different Lord and vision of life. In our time, Christians can be greatly nourished and strengthened by a similar experience.

And so I strongly commend this program to you. Not only is it an exceedingly fine tool for communicating an emerging vision of Christianity, but, even more importantly, it is a means for embodying it.

– Marcus Borg

PREFACE

THE ORIGINS OF THIS EXPERIENTIAL GUIDE

In August 2003, after 24 years of program development and leadership at Naramata Centre, a conference and retreat facility run by the United Church of Canada, it was time for me to move on to a new challenge. I was very fortunate to be called to fulltime ministry at Penticton United Church, where the focus of my work was to be on faith formation particularly through small group ministry.

I had been aware for some time of the popularity of the Alpha Course, a program of exploration into key issues of the Christian faith, which originated in Britain and which has caught on all across North America. I checked it out and discovered that it was based on a conservative Christian theology, one in which I did not feel at home. People in the church where I work were asking about the Alpha Course and some were even attending the program at other churches in our town. I had a sense that people were not only interested but also hungry for the opportunity presented by Alpha.

Just as I was arriving at Penticton United Church, Marcus Borg's new book, *The Heart of Christianity*, was arriving in bookstores. When I read it, I discovered that, in his presentation of an "earlier" Christianity and an "emerging" Christianity, he was describing the difference between the Alpha Course and the course I wanted to offer people in our congregation. The problem was that the latter didn't exist. So, in January of 2004, I began to create and to offer, week-by-week, an experiential program based on the 11 chapters of *The Heart of Christianity*. The 12th week was a session that brought closure to the learning community, enabled people to draw together their learning from the whole program, and evaluated various elements of the program and all that we had achieved together.

The program, as I offered it between January and March 2004, held the interest of 36 people for 12 weeks. Not bad for a moderate-sized United Church congregation whose members are involved in all kinds of evening community activities! Folks at Wood Lake Books got wind of the enterprise and began conversations with me about the possibility of publishing the course as an experiential "encounter" with the Borg book.

The summer of 2004 included many hours of translating my own process notes into an accessible program for facilitators in Christian faith communities of the kind that would welcome Marcus Borg's theology and teaching with the same enthusiasm as I do. What remarkable gifts he has brought to my life! I had the privilege of inviting him to Naramata Centre on a number of occasions, to teach courses based on some of his wonderful books: *Meeting Jesus Again for the First Time*; *The God We Never Knew*; and *The Meaning of Jesus: Two Visions*, which he coauthored with N. T. Wright.

In my estimation, Marcus Borg is among the very finest of biblical scholars, theologians, and faith teachers. His capacity to connect the faith insights of scholars to the remarkable ordinariness of our everyday living is extraordinary. No wonder his teaching calendar is full two or three years ahead and that the invitations are coming from beyond North America, too.

In that same spirit of generosity and commitment that has him traveling extensively to respond to people's enthusiasm for his writing and teaching, he has been extremely welcoming of our initiative to extend the power of the book through an experiential learning program. I appreciate his trust in encouraging us to proceed to publication along a very tight timeline. It feels like an awesome responsibility to be translating such a remarkable text into the language of experiential learning.

I hope that, as you facilitate the educational designs of this course, you will find that the processes are congruent with the spirit and intent of Marcus' book and that you will be transformed, as I have been, in your encounter with *The Heart of Christianity*.

INTRODUCTION

WHEN A BOOK IS THE STARTING POINT...

What do you do with a book that is given as the "text for the course"?

I recognize a tendency in myself to want to "master the text" or "learn the book." I suspect that this is a leftover from school days, when there were questions at the end of each chapter to be answered, and when success meant being able to respond accurately to each question. Such a methodology assumes a particular approach to learning that is more about accurately passing on information and ideas from the author than it is about stimulating thought and insight in the learner.

It would be possible to write that kind of study guide for *The Heart of Christianity* (HarperSanFrancisco, 2004). The book is packed with ideas and, if Marcus Borg is anything, he is a master of clear presentation. It would be very easy to write 20 questions for each chapter and to engage groups of adults in responding to those questions:

- What are the three central assertions in Borg's faith?
- What are the five characteristics of Borg's pre-Easter Jesus?
- What does the word "salvation" mean to Borg?

If that's the kind of study guide you are looking for, go no further with this one!

The approach I take is to assume that each person will purchase their own copy of the *Heart of Christianity* and will come to the session having read the given chapter. Experience tells me that they will be highly stimulated by what Borg has written and that they will be eager to talk with others about Borg's presentation and their personal response to him. They will also be keen to hear what others make of ideas that to them may seem anything from mildly challenging to wildly outrageous. A very typical response to Borg's teaching is, "Why didn't someone tell me this before? I needed to hear this years ago!"

I trust people to deal with the content of the book. What I'm most interested in working with is the energy of people's response to ideas that connect powerfully to the most important concerns of their lives. An accurate regurgitation of Borg's teaching is not nearly as promising or meaningful as an energetic engagement at the place where his heart-offered teaching elicits a heartfelt response from adults in a group.

This is not a traditional study guide, then. It's a catalyst for group process. It's a resource to help adults find language and pathways that will enable them to explore the matters that are of greatest consequence in their lives. It's a catalogue of possibilities for helping groups of adults to frame the experiences of their lives in ways that make sense to them as citizens of the 21st century. It's a pathway into the classroom of Marcus Borg, a biblical scholar who knows that, ultimately, it is the truth within our own hearts that we must each know and name.

NOTES ON FACILITATING THIS PROGRAM

Using the DVD

The DVD included in this book contains a video guide for leaders. Under the menu item "For Leaders" you will find an introduction to the program, as well as 12 video clips, in which I offer advice on how to approach each of the 12 sessions. I highly recommend that you view the relevant leader's clip prior to each session, as part of your planning. The DVD also contains six clips of Marcus Borg that can be shown to group participants. More about this later.

Respecting the participation of group members

As a facilitator of experiential learning, your task is to lead people to a creative and, potentially, transformative encounter with the topic at hand.

Think of yourself as one who respectfully "accompanies" participants on their journey of faith and spiritual formation. Think of yourself as one who sets aside what you think are the "best" or "right" ideas or answers, and who stays fully present to the truth that is being expressed by each participant. Think of yourself as a midwife of new awareness in each person in the group, including yourself.

The kind of environment you want to create is one in which people feel affirmed in their participation, not judged; one in which people feel safe to take risks, not "shut down" by fear of giving the "wrong" answer. You will create such an environment not only through your words, but also through your body language. You can express respect, openness, and trust as powerfully with your non-verbal communication as you can with your words. The most effective way to ensure that you communicate in that way is to carry in you a belief of this kind: *I am here to give guidance to this group as we learn together. I am open to being changed as much as I hope they are. I respect the capacity of each member of this group to be responsible for their own learning. They do not have to accept what I believe or what the author of the book believes. Their journey of faith and spirit is unique, and never to be repeated. I feel gratitude that I can be part of each person's unfolding story.*

Take time to write that kind of statement for yourself. It needs to be true for you: your words, not mine. What do you really believe about yourself as a facilitator?

A final word about respect: as I lead these sessions, I am constantly amazed and blessed by the new insights that tumble out of each session into my own awareness. In other words, this process is also transforming me. We, as facilitators, are as vulnerable to learning as everyone else in the group, even though we have this special responsibility of leadership. Nothing will express respect more powerfully than respecting our own evolving awareness in matters such as spirit, mystery, faith, and heart. What a calling! What a blessing!

Making the program designs work for you

I'm sure that if all the facilitators who will use this study were to stand on a line from "very experienced" to "just starting," we would have a very long continuum of group leadership experience. This study has been written with that whole continuum in mind. That means that skilled facilitators will look at it and say, "That's not what *I* would say if I were giving directions for this activity; I would say this…" Less-experienced facilitators will say, "What a relief that someone has given me an idea of what to say here, how to introduce this activity…"

I believe that I am giving you enough content, whatever your level of skill and experience, to make this study work effectively for you. It does mean, however, that you need to spend time with the printed design ahead of each session to do these five things:

1. Make the connection in your own mind between the chapter, as written by Marcus Borg, and the intent and main emphasis of the session.
2. Decide, from all that is offered in the design, what the priorities are for *you,* now that you are getting to know the particular group you are facilitating.
3. Add to the design program elements that you think are missing and that you think would be important for you and your group.
4. Decide what words you will use to introduce parts of the process and to bridge from one element to another.
5. Estimate roughly the amount of time that you want to allocate to each part of the process.

Words in bold face

It seems to me that the most effective way of conveying to you what my intention is at any place in the program is to give you the kind of words that I would use and leave you free to use those words or your own version of them. The text in bold face in each session offers the kind of words I would tend to use at that stage in the process.

The truth is that I will use different words every time I lead the course, depending on a wide variety of circumstances:

- how well the group members know one another and me,
- how much time we have,
- how well people seem to be responding to what's going on,
- the general mood of the group,
- and a perceived connection to something that just happened in the previous activity.

I expect and hope that this is also true for you and that you will vary the wording of your introductions, transition statements, and instructions depending on your reading of the group and its members.

The other thing to say is that I much prefer to give instructions and to lead things, such as opening and closing worship, without reading from a text. As I said in the previous section ("Making the program designs work for you"), a lot will depend on your level of experience in group facilitation. The more experience you have, the more likely you are to let go of the script and to improvise based on what's happening and the direction in which you want the group to move.

Words not in bold face

The text that is *not* in bold face is either instruction to you, biblical text, lists of supplies or words related to an activity that you will be giving the group.

Paired conversations

Early in a session, I often have people go into pairs for some quick warm-up conversations. It's a great way to break the ice and to have people talking with one another about something they are bringing with them to the session, or about something related to the topic of emphasis. Typically the conversations take three to five minutes depending on the topic given. I like to have people stand for these, moving quickly from one partner to the next. I use a Tibetan bell to signal that the time for the conversation is coming to an end; that way I don't have to shout to be heard above the babble of conversation. I will suggest topics for the conversations, but you can choose topics that you think will work well for your particular group.

Name tags

Working with a group of over 30 people, I asked people to wear name tags for the first few sessions. In a group of 16 or less, I would not use name tags, but I would build in ways for people to get to know the names of group members.

Living the questions

It's inevitable that a book that presents as many significant ideas as Marcus Borg's does will generate all kinds of questions. Questions are not necessarily things that have to be answered. We tend to think that way because we live in a culture that values productivity, and answering questions seems like a productive thing to do! It is helpful, sometimes, to think of questions as wonderings, as indicators of where a person is in their own process of growth and learning. Encourage people to bring their questions to the surface and to express them.

Here's a great way to do that in a group setting. Have a sheet of newsprint and some different colored markers available in the meeting space. In each session, encourage people to write their current questions on this "Question Page." "Here's what people are wondering about," you will say periodically. Sometimes, you might take one of the questions and fit it into your process: "I just noticed this question that someone wrote up last week and I think it's connected to what we're talking about here. What do you think?"

Life is really more about "living the questions" than "finding the answers." This practice of "surfacing the questions" is a very appropriate one, because it is fully in tune with the theology of *The Heart of Christianity*. I can just hear Marcus Borg saying something like,

"I don't know, but it's a great question. Let's note that and come back to it later."

Asking for feedback

It seems like an obvious thing to do, but, for one reason or another, it often gets neglected. On a course that could go for 12 weeks, there's a lot of potential for adapting to the needs, interests, and preferences of the participants. There are some natural places in the program to do a kind of mini-evaluation. Right after Session 5 – as you come to the end of "Part One: Seeing the Christian Tradition Again" – would be an obvious place to step back and ask people, "How's it going…is this working for you…what would make it better…what would you like less of/more of…?"

You may be hesitant to open yourself to the possibility that people don't like everything you are doing. But it's worth taking the risk, so that you can also hear how much they appreciate your leadership!

Going with the flow

There will be times when you know intuitively that it's more important to stay with a key issue than to forge ahead with the next part of the process. Knowing when to do that is part of the art of facilitation. In the context of this particular study, you will likely find yourself wondering quite often, "Should I let this discussion go on, or should I propose that we move on to the next thing." In making this judgment, here are some of the kinds of questions you might ask yourself.

– Is this a matter of "head" or "heart"? There is a place for talking about ideas, but the power of this program is in honoring the heart, in valuing the lived experience of each member of the group.

– Is this matter that is pulling the attention of the group something that we just *have* to take time to speak about? Is it truly the place where this group might learn the most in this session?

 - If we spend time on this matter, will it mean that something else
   of equal or greater importance, such good closure of the session or
   attention to another important complementary topic, will be lost at
   a cost?

THE "THIN PLACES" OF FAITH EDUCATION: LEARNING TOGETHER AS A SACRED ACT

In Session 8, you will find significant emphasis put on the metaphor of
thin places. A thin place, as Marcus Borg explains, is one of those places
where the veil between the visible world of our ordinary experience and
the sacred presence of God momentarily lifts. "God shines through
everything."

The arena of experiential learning is one of those places of human
interaction that offers, very richly, an awareness of God's presence in our
lives, in our relationships. This is especially the case when the subject
matter of the experiential learning process is the human heart, the life of
faith, and the desire for passionate belief.

Knowing this to be true, I create an environment of learning in which
"thin-place experiences" are encouraged, welcomed, and sustained. I do
this because the presence of the Spirit is ultimately the most powerful
source of transformation and learning in our lives, and because deeper
connection to Spirit, to the sacred, is often the thing that program
participants most want in their lives. They really *do* want to open their
hearts and to be more aware of God's presence as holy companion on
their way.

There are many things an educator can do that will contribute to the
creation of a setting for sacred learning in community. You will become
aware of some of these when you use this resource with a group.

1. **Prepare the space in which you are meeting as if it were a
    sanctuary for learning and transformation.** Set out the furniture
    with care, imagining and anticipating the learning processes
    that will unfold in that space. It makes an enormous difference

to people when they arrive in a room that has been prepared for them. Whether they are conscious of it or not, the fact that the place of learning has been "set" for them makes a huge difference in their capacity to be present and open to the possibilities of interaction and learning. Think carefully about the right configuration of chairs based on the learning processes for the session. For example, when I'm working with a large group and I know that I will often have people in groups of four, I set the chairs that way so that as people arrive they move naturally into that configuration and begin to interact and feel included.

2. **Take care in placing and setting the table that will function as a sacred center for the group,** whether you are sitting in a circle or in some other arrangement. I know that as the sessions unfold the objects that I put on the table will come to have special symbolic meaning. These items will carry the memory of the group's learning. You might choose a distinctive candle to accompany the group through all 12 sessions. Perhaps the candle is set on a rock in a bowl of water so that when reference is made to water in the opening of some sessions, the light and the water are there in relation to one another. I will have some additional water in a pottery jug on the table to add to the bowl of water at the right moment in the opening time. You might have the table covered with a piece of fabric the color of which will represent the season of the church year in which the session is happening.

3. **Use a resonant bell, or other harmonious sound maker, to signal** when it's time for people to wrap up their conversation and move their attention back to the group, or for any other time when you need to signal a change in process unobtrusively. My four-inch wide Tibetan bell with its wooden striker has become an essential tool of my leadership. Sometimes I will use it as a simple marker of transition; for

example, as I move a group from a time of prayer into a time of giving instruction. I love to find ways of directing people in a learning process that minimize the use of my voice, not because my voice is becoming tired or ineffective, but because words engage people's brains in a very different way than bells do. Words, for any number of reasons, can be intrusive and interruptive. The sound of a bell, especially when the meaning of the ring has been announced ahead of time, can be not only clear and concise, but spiritually affirming.

4. **Lead the session not only as educational process, but as worship.**
    Think of yourself not only as teacher, but as an artist of the sacred. You will notice that each session in the program opens with a time of worship that includes the candle, scripture, the water, words of welcome and some reference to the focus of the week. There are also suggestions for worshipful closings. In addition to these moments of worship, you may discover other times of spontaneous worship emerging in the course of the session and you might choose to use a symbol, a prayer, an invitation to silence, or a sacred song to enhance the sense of the sacred.

5. **Treat transitions from one part of the session to the next as an opportunity to offer care to the participants you are guiding.**
    I don't want people to be jarred by a transition from one kind of activity or topic to a very different one, so I anticipate what is coming up and find ways to create a bridge:

- through a choice of words that verbally build the bridge,
- through a simple sound, like the bell ringing, which signals the change,
- through having people do something physical, such as changing seating arrangement, stretching, or moving,
- through singing a hymn or song together,
- and through gently introducing a piece of background music that anticipates in mood or word what is coming up.

THE PATTERN OF EACH SESSION

Every session will follow the same format, which will become familiar to you. The length of each part of the session will vary from week to week.

Intend

- You will find the intent or purpose of each session presented at the beginning of the outline. It's there for your guidance. You may share elements of it with the program participants at any time that seems right to you. Some people really like to have a heads-up on what's included in the session; it helps them to relax, knowing that things are well in hand.

- My preference is to wait and to share my intention for the session after the opening, or even after the connecting time. I think it's good to allow people that settling in and connecting time before going into the overview of what's planned. They can pay attention better after they've had a chance to feel included and reconnected with the group.

- The wording at the beginning of this section always says, "Outcomes for this session include the following..." This indicates that this is not an exclusive list of outcomes, but enough to give a general sense of the overall thrust and focus of the session.

- All of the outcome statements begin with an active "...ing" word to convey a sense of the program as dynamic and energetic.

Prepare

- This section outlines what you need to do as facilitator in order to be ready to lead the session.

- The outline includes preparation of materials, resources, and a list of things to be photocopied, where necessary.

- I advise checking this list a session in advance to give yourself time to round up items that might not be readily at hand (such as clay, for example).

Welcome

- This section provides a sentence you can write, prior to the session, on a newsprint sheet, which you should place in a spot that is clearly visible to people as they arrive.
- This will include the word "Welcome," the name and number of the session, and a topic of conversation or an activity for participants to pursue while others are arriving.

Open

- This section provides a prayerful opening to the session, which always includes the lighting of a candle on a central table and an invitation for people to drink from the water provided as they feel the need.
- The opening usually includes a passage of scripture related to the focus of the week.
- The opening makes reference in some way to the theme of the session.

Connect

- This section provides an intentional opportunity for people to meet with one another, sometimes in pairs, often in small groups.
- The connecting time addresses the need for people to feel acknowledged and included in the group, not just once, but at every session. When people do not feel included, it is unlikely that they will learn much, especially in an environment of experiential learning.
- The ways that people are invited to connect vary greatly from week to week.

Engage

- Once people feel connected, they can engage in the meaty issues of the session.

- In most sessions, there are three kinds of activity for engaging with the theme.
- The different activities of this section are not intended to be "options," although if you run out of time to do everything this might be the section from which to drop something; often, the activities are sequential, building on one another or addressing in a logical way the key issues that Borg addresses in that chapter.
- A DVD has been included in this book, which includes clips of Marcus Borg that can be shown in Sessions 1, 3, 5, 9, 10, and 11, as well as images of Jesus which can be shown in Session 5.
- An attempt has been made to include a wide variety of activities in this section and to appeal to the diversity of ways that people learn.

Anticipate

- This section looks ahead to the next session and proposes ways for people to prepare themselves for it.
- Sometimes, it picks up on the focus of the present week and makes a bridge to the emphasis of the next week.
- On some occasions, it is very precise about asking participants to bring something or to do something in preparation.

Close

- In the same spirit as the opening, the closing offers sacred words and actions to bring the session to a worshipful end.
- The closing always includes the paraphrase of the Prayer of Jesus – a kind of ongoing prayer practice for the community. If this prayer or version of the prayer seems inappropriate for your group, please substitute with a different one that feels right for you and your group.
- The closing sometimes includes a ritual that invites active participation from the group members.

- You should feel free to shape the closing to be in tune with the sacred path that the group has walked in that session; if what is proposed feels out of sync with what has emerged in the group or with the mood of the session, do something that *is* in sync.
- You could always use a song or a hymn as a summary of the session; make use of musicians and singers if you have them.

LENGTH OF SESSIONS & RHYTHMS OF LEARNING

Each session is designed to be no longer than two hours and fifteen minutes in length. This means that an evening session might run from 7:00 to 9:15. You might find that most sessions can be completed without rushing in two hours. I believe that this length of session accommodates people's capacity to focus on matters of substance without becoming too tired. I prefer to fall short of using the full time and have people leave a little early, rather than rush to get done on time and have to go a little over.

When it comes to predicting the time an activity will take in an experiential educational process, it really is difficult to be exact. You just never know when some special interest in a topic or an activity will be sparked and will take more time than you anticipated. The task of the facilitator is to guide the group's use of the time, allowing the potential of an activity to be realized, while exercising judgment in making space for the diversity of activities and topics to be addressed.

It is important, therefore, that you are familiar with the design of the session before leading it so that you can make a judgment ahead of time about the elements of the program that have high priority for you. Then, if you find yourself running out of time for everything that remains, you can make an informed judgment about what to leave out.

Here are the principles by which I operate, consciously and unconsciously, when making decisions about content and timing.

1. **Drop elements from the program, or shorten them, rather than rush the process.** When people are rushed, they begin to feel

things such as anxiety, resistance, confusion, and irritation. As soon as that happens, the quality and focus of their learning decreases. It is far better for the participants to learn fewer things and remain grounded, focused, and connected.

2. **Make sure that there is a sense of closure both at the end of each part of the process as well as at the end of each session.** There is the same sense of satisfaction in experiencing clear transitions and clear endings in an educational process as there is in music. Leadership of experiential education is, indeed, an art. People will respond with openness and energy when you lead as a sacred artist, honoring the human need for and awareness of openings, transitions, rhythms, and closure.

3. **If you have to let something go, opt for leaving in those things that will maintain a variety of experience within the session.** You will notice a considerable diversity of activities in each session: discussion in various configurations; personal reflection and writing, as well as sharing with others; creative activities as well as meditative ones; and so on. In addition to having a variety of topics within a session, it is important in experiential learning to offer a variety of modes of learning.

THE SIZE AND DYNAMICS OF THE GROUP

When I first led this course, I imagined that I would attract a group of about 12 people and that we would spend a good deal of our time in a circle of discussion, breaking out into groups of two, three, or four for various interactive processes. I was quite taken aback when 36 people registered and stayed for the whole 12 sessions! That response dramatically changed the dynamics of the program and my role in relation to the group.

Options

These are the two main options I see in terms of group size and experiential process.

1. **Small group: up to 16 participants**

   The group is seated in a circle and you facilitate a good deal of group sharing and discussion. During each session, there are times for people to break off into groups of two, three, or four, depending on the nature of the exercise. I think that an ideal group size is 12: small enough to generate a sense of trust and intimacy, yet large enough to offer some diversity of experience and thought. As a facilitator, once the group grows beyond 12 members, I begin to become less effective in tracking the individuals and the group.

2. **Large group: over 16 participants**

   Once you have 16–20 people in the circle, dynamics change and you have to make much more use of small group configurations. This is because there are just too many people for the "airtime" to be shared between them all, and for the goals of the session to be achieved. It also becomes more challenging for people who find it difficult to speak in a group. I like the practice of setting chairs in groups of four before the session, clearly establishing those groupings as people arrive. In those configurations, people begin to check in with one another immediately. That's their small group for the session. You can still have large group sharing with those groups of four still in place.

At the first session of the program, I make it clear that these groups of four are the norm for the whole program. I also get people to agree to a practice of changing group membership every week. As people arrive, they not only have a choice about where to sit, but with whom to sit. Some people will undertake this as the challenge of seeing if, in the course of 12 sessions, they can be in a group with everyone else at least once!

Choice

Your relationship with the group will be quite different depending on whether you have a large or small group. When I'm working with a group of 30 people, I will not know as much as I would like to about what's going on for each person. You might decide to limit registration for the program to 16 and run two sessions, if necessary.

On the other hand, a lot of energy will be generated by a group of 30 people coming together to engage with the issues that matter most to them. The biggest payoff in using the groups-of-four model is the sense of intimacy and trust that is created. People express great appreciation for the opportunity to share in the intimacy of a group of four from week to week. It's something that doesn't happen anywhere else in their lives; they are truly fed by the experience and come back as much for the small group as for the content of the program.

THE MEETING SPACE

Location

Because this is a small group experience, you might be meeting in any number of locations: a church parlor, a classroom, a member's living room, the church sanctuary. The choice of space will depend a lot on the size of the group and on whether you are going to have the group in one circle or in a configuration of fours.

Assuming it's available, don't dismiss too quickly the church sanctuary as a meeting space. I'm fortunate that, when I move the altar table, there is room between the front row of pews and the organ for a circle of chairs that includes up to ten groups of four. There's something about engaging in the matters of this book while being in the atmosphere a sanctuary can provide that adds much to the experience.

Table

Place a table at the center of the group regardless of the configuration you have chosen. On the table, place a candle and provide a space for other symbols that might be introduced in the session. Sometimes when a symbol is introduced in one session I like to keep it on the table in subsequent sessions as a symbolic reminder of an earlier related moment in our exploration.

Water

Rather than interrupt a two-and-a-half-hour session with a break, I prefer to have drinking water available for people to take at any time they need it. Using water rather than other beverages is simple and effective, as it emphasizes the sacred and basic quality of our relationships and of our discussion.

Newsprint

Some sessions will require the use of a flip chart and newsprint. When needed, this will be included in the "Prepare" section at the beginning of the session outline.

Sound

Audibility is probably the biggest drawback to using a sanctuary and having people spread out in groups of four. So when I use the sanctuary with a large group, I have a handheld wireless microphone available, both for myself to address the group and for others to report in from their group discussions.

SESSION

1

THE HEART OF CHRISTIANITY
IN A TIME OF CHANGE

INTEND

(This is for your guidance: you can share aspects of it with the group
at any time that seems right to you.)

Outcomes for this session include the following:
- ❑ laying the groundwork for the 12-week program;
- ❑ meeting and beginning to get to know one another;
- ❑ being clear about purpose, principles, and schedule;
- ❑ introducing a way of being together in these sessions;
- ❑ beginning to share faith stories;
- ❑ hearing the questions, wonderings, and concerns of this group;
- ❑ practicing listening to one another with openness and compassion;
- ❑ engaging with some of the ideas that Borg presents in this first chapter;
- ❑ identifying some of the important questions that we hope to address in this journey;
- ❑ hearing scripture that addresses our beginning of this program;
- ❑ living into a powerful metaphor of our spiritual path: the unending conversation.

PREPARE

Have a DVD player and TV or data projector ready to play the Marcus Borg clip "The Emerging Paradigm," should you wish to use this option.

❏ Place water and drinking glasses on a side table that is easily accessible to all.

❏ Place a candle on a central table; have matches ready.

❏ Place a loaf of bread on the central table and some rice cakes for people who cannot eat bread.

❏ Make copies of the paraphrase of "The Prayer of Jesus," by Jim Cotter. (page 45).

❏ Make copies of "Experiencing the Heart of Christianity: Purpose and Principles" (page 42), "Two Paradigms: A Tale of Two Christianities" (page 44), and "The Unending Conversation" (page 43) and have them ready to hand out during the session.

❏ Prepare your own list of things that you have received from the tradition of which you have been a part; such as the Bible, God, Jesus, creeds, practices, ritual, and so on. You will find my list as a model in the "Engage" section, below.

❏ Prepare a schedule for the course that shows the date and name of each session and the liturgical season(s) in which you are meeting. Make copies of this schedule for each person.

WELCOME

Make sure the following words of welcome and instruction are written on newsprint and displayed in a spot where everyone can read them as they arrive:

Welcome to Session 1: The Heart of Christianity in a Time of Change
Please find a chair and introduce yourself to another person in the group. Talk about what attracted you to this program.

OPEN

Welcome to this community of exploration and learning. A place has been prepared here for you.

There is light here in the flame of this candle. (Light the candle.)

The light has come into the darkness and the darkness has not put out that light.

There is water for refreshment. (Indicate the presence of water and glasses.)

The living water flows abundantly for all and is here to be shared in community.

There is a company of searchers, who will go with you on this journey of rediscovery.

The company includes people like you who know both fear and love and who seek to live with courage and passion.

In each of our sessions, a passage of scripture will be included in the opening time. In this first session, we will hear a story of two people who long ago went on a journey quite similar to the one on which we are embarking.

Hear this story of people accompanying one another in a journey of uncertainty, even as they hold on to their desire to be passionate believers.

Luke 24:13–35

Now on that same day two of them were going to a village called Emmaus, about seven miles from Jerusalem, and talking with each other about all these things that had happened.

While they were talking and discussing, Jesus himself came near and went with them, but their eyes were kept from recognizing him.

And he said to them, "What are you discussing with each other while you walk along?"

They stood still, looking sad. Then one of them, whose name was Cleopas, answered him, "Are you the only stranger in Jerusalem who does not know the things that have taken place there in these days?"

He asked them, "What things?"

They replied, "The things about Jesus of Nazareth, who was a prophet mighty in deed and word before God and all the people, and how our chief priests and leaders handed him over to be condemned to death and crucified him. But we had hoped that he was the one to redeem Israel. Yes, and besides all this, it is now the third day since these things took place. Moreover, some women of our group astounded us. They were at the tomb early this morning, and when they did not find his body there, they came back and told us that they had indeed seen a vision of angels who said that he was alive. Some of those who were with us went to the tomb and found it just as the women had said; but they did not see him."

Then he said to them, "Oh, how foolish you are, and how slow of heart to believe all that the prophets have declared! Was it not necessary that the Messiah should suffer these things and then enter into his glory?" Then beginning with Moses and all the prophets, he interpreted to them the things about himself in all the scriptures.

As they came near the village to which they were going, he walked ahead as if he were going on. But they urged him strongly, saying, "Stay with us, because it is almost evening and the day is now nearly over." So he went in to stay with them.

When he was at the table with them, he took bread, blessed and broke it, and gave it to them. Then their eyes were opened, and they recognized him; and he vanished from their sight.

They said to each other, "Were not our hearts burning within us while he was talking to us on the road, while he was opening the scriptures to us?"

That same hour they got up and returned to Jerusalem; and they found the eleven and their companions gathered together. They were saying, "The Lord has risen indeed, and he has appeared to Simon!" Then they told what had happened on the road, and how he had been made known to them in the breaking of the bread.

You will notice that the storyteller, Luke, tells us that one of the travelers in this story was named Cleopas. We are not told the name of the other traveler.

It is reassuring to know the names of those with whom we travel and to speak our own names in this community of learners.

Let's go around the circle and hear the names of those who have gathered here today. Say your name, and we will all say it together as an acknowledgement of your presence here.

Each person says his or her name. Everyone else responds by saying aloud together that person's name.

CONNECT

Paired Conversations (See page 14, "Notes on Facilitating this Program.")

One of the key elements of this program is interactive conversation, sometimes in groups of three or four, but right now in pairs. You will have three quick conversations, of about three or four minutes each, *with three different people,* on topics I will give you.

Conversation 1:

Please turn to a person next to you for your first conversation and talk together about this:

If I weren't here on a *(Monday evening)*, I would be...

Conversation 2:

Now turn to the person on your other side for the next conversation:

When I here the word "Christianity", I have this reaction (these reactions)...

Conversation 3:

Now move across the circle to someone you haven't spoken with yet, perhaps not even met before...

Based on what attracted me here, I think that this course could make this kind of difference at this time in my life...

You'll notice that you'll begin a lot of conversations in this program, some that you might like more time to finish. It will be up to you to find ways of pursuing those conversations beyond the session time.

Concerning the conversations you just had, there will be many occasions during these 12 sessions to talk about all things Christian, including your reaction to the word "Christianity."

Let's take a moment now to pick up on some of the things you may have said or heard in the third conversation, about what attracted you to this course and what your hopes for it are.

Tell me what you hope might come from this course and I'll record what I hear on the newsprint sheet.

Record responses only once, even though you might acknowledge a repeated response when it is offered more than once.

When it feels as though you have received all the responses, call an end to the listing and make any personal response you might feel is appropriate to the list of "hopes" you have received. There might, for example, be hopes expressed that you know will not be fulfilled in the course of this program. Better to be clear about that right from the start, so that people aren't left waiting for something that will never come.

Hand out copies of the page, "Experiencing the Heart of Christianity: Purpose and Principles."

Having heard some of the things that attracted you to the course and that you hope might come from it, I want to be clear about the purpose of the program and some of the principles by which we will order our time as a community of learners. Take a couple of minutes in silence to read this page before we go on.

When people have finished reading…

First of all, is there anything on this page that's unclear to you? (Clarify as needed.) **Is there anything that you could not live with and that you would not be willing to accept as a principle for our life together as a learning community?** (Negotiate changes and additions as necessary.)

At some point each week, I will give an overview of what is planned for the session. It likely won't be right at the beginning, but it will be before we get into the main learning process of the session. I'll say a few words right now about what I have planned for this session. (See "Intend.")

ENGAGE

In this chapter, Marcus Borg introduces us to the metaphor of "the unending conversation," which he owes to Kenneth Burke, an American intellectual of the 20th century. We are going to use this metaphor as a way of previewing the journey we are going on in these 12 sessions. Here's a handout that introduces the metaphor, as well as the framework of exploration we will use for about the next 45 minutes.

Hand out the copies of "The Unending Conversation" and introduce the framework.

As we use this metaphor of the unending conversation, we will be influenced by three key words: RECEIVING, INTERPRETING, and ALLOWING.

As an additional option, and if you have access to a DVD player and TV or data projector, you may wish to show the Marcus Borg video clip, "The Emerging Paradigm."

Receiving

In this model, "receiving" refers to what we have been given within our tradition, which for most of us will be the Christian tradition. This would include such things as the Bible, God, Jesus, creeds, practices, ritual, and so on.

What have you received from your tradition?

These are the kinds of things I recognize have come to me from the tradition of which I have been a part since my birth: (The examples below are from my own life. Ideally, you will have prepared your own list and have it ready to share with the group.)

  - a love of biblical story (from images by artists, drama, storytellers, illustrated books),

- a profound sense of the sacred in all things (from choir experiences, from priestly father, from childhood in rural England),
- a conviction of the love of God who cares and is involved and blesses us with the freedom of choice,
- an ever-unfolding relationship with the person of Jesus,
- a dynamic faith, never static, always unfolding,
- the rhythm of the church year – seasons coming and going, the repetition, living the faith story,
- the freedom to challenge and think creatively from writers and scholars such as John Robinson, Mary Jo Leddy, Diarmuid O'Murchu, and Marcus Borg,
- the inspiration of people who live their conviction with passion,
- the love of language (King James version, psalms, poetic passages, Book of Common Prayer),
- a tendency to think of people in biblical story outside their own cultural context, living in ways more akin to modern North America than ancient Palestine. (This isn't necessarily positive; in fact, there can be a number which are about negative impact.)

Take five minutes on your own and identify personal examples of what you have received from the Christian tradition. If you are not able to identify anything, for whatever reason, then let that be your response.

Move into groups of four. (Since this is the first session and people are new to this group, it might be best to establish groups by numbering around the circle. This also gets people interacting with people they might not otherwise have approached.)

Each person will have two or three minutes to share with the group some of what they have received from their tradition. You have a total of ____ minutes. Please share the time so that everyone who wants to speak will have a chance to do so.

After everyone in the group has had a chance to speak…

In your groups, take a moment to talk together about what you noticed from the sharing that people have just done. There might have been some recurring themes, a blend of both positive and negative influences, and some surprises.

Now we will move on to the second stage of the process related to The Unending Conversation.

Interpreting

In this model, "interpreting" refers to the process of thinking in new ways and for a new time about what we have received from the tradition.

In this book, Marcus Borg encourages us to interpret the Christian tradition we have received in a way that recognizes our present cultural context, without diminishing the power of that tradition. You will have already noticed in your reading of this chapter that Marcus Borg presents this reinterpretation as a shift from what he calls an "earlier Christianity" to an "emerging Christianity."

Hand out the copies of "Two Paradigms: A Tale of Two Christianities."

This handout summarizes, in four categories, the main distinctions between these two different ways of living the Christian "Way": an "earlier" way and an "emerging" way. You might think of this page as an overview of the central idea of Borg's book. We will be exploring these ideas more fully in the next four sessions of the course, but right now we're just getting a sense of the main idea that Marcus Borg presents.

Make sure people have time to read the handout and to ask questions for clarification. Don't worry if you don't have an answer for all the questions. By the time you come to the end of Session 5, everyone will have had an opportunity to come to a full understanding of the words and ideas presented here.

Given this change that Borg is proposing, what questions does it raise for you?

Go back into your groups of four and list the questions that come to mind as you think about this paradigm shift in Christianity. Have one member of your group record these questions.

We are going to hear the questions that you recorded in your groups as a litany of wondering. We will make no attempt to respond to the questions at this time. As the sessions go by, we will live many of these questions, responding to them as they emerge.

Allowing

In this model, "allowing" refers to the spiritual practices that will make room for the Spirit to be active in the deepening of your faith throughout this entire program.

As we begin this faith exploration together, we recognize that it is both communal and solitary. We will be with one another during these sessions, but in the time between, you will read the book and reflect on what you have read, what you have experienced, and what we have discussed.

What ways might you intentionally use to open yourself to the voice of the Spirit, which comes both from that which is "given" and that which is "emerging"? I am inviting you to think about spiritual practice as a feature of your time between sessions in this program. For example, you might consider such things as journaling, meditation, a creative art, songwriting, and prayer. Take a moment to talk to one other person about any spiritual practices that appeal to you, as you think about how you will accompany your own spirit during this program of faith renewal.

ANTICIPATE

In chapter 2 of *The Heart of Christianity*, Marcus Borg defines faith as "loving God and all that God loves." As you go through the week ahead, pay attention to God's world by asking yourself, "What is it that God loves right here, right now?"

CLOSE

In our opening time, we heard the story of the two travelers who only recognized the third traveler when he broke bread with them. This process that you have set out on today will be a journey of recognition and revelation. Let us break bread and share it together, both as a sign of our trust in the revealing power of the Spirit and also as a sign of our willingness to accompany one another on the journey. As we offer bread to one another, we will say, "Bread for the journey."

Offer the bread to one another.

As we come to the end of this time, we will say a form of the Prayer of Jesus, which we will use at the end of each session. It is the one thing that will remain constant within a program that is full of variety. This paraphrase was written by Jim Cotter. Let us pray together.

Experiencing the Heart of Christianity

PURPOSE

To gather in Christian community,
allowing ourselves to be challenged, taught, and inspired by Marcus Borg,
so that we might pursue our way of faith with passion, heart, and intellect.

PRINCIPLES

1. Even though our focus is study and discussion, we are first and foremost a community of faith. We will live our 12 sessions together as an intentional community, including in our life together prayer, ritual, hospitality, and accompaniment. There will be an obvious congruence between what we are addressing in the book and how we meet together.

2. Assuming that in this community of learners there is a diversity of people in terms of faith practice, biblical and theological knowledge, association with the Christian tradition, commitment to the Way of Jesus, and relationship with God, we will practice disciplines of inclusiveness, non-judgment, and openness to learning from differences.

3. Every session will stand on its own so that if participants happen to miss a session, they can spend time in personal study of that chapter and not miss the content, even though they will miss the community learning process.

4. We will exercise a discipline of focusing on the content of the chapter of the week, not jumping ahead to future chapters, even when there may be a connection to the discussion of the session. The program will be cumulative; as we go, we will be aware of a growing body of communal learning to which we can make reference.

5. Marcus Borg is the one providing the shape and content of the course. Within the framework of concepts, ideas, and story that he provides, we will add our own content. The facilitator will take responsibility for the process of each session, inviting participants to make requests, give feedback, and take initiatives as appropriate.

6. Inevitably, as we consider matters of such significance to our lives, we may find ourselves wishing to be in conversation with a faith or spiritual companion outside the session time. Participants are encouraged to follow through on this whenever they feel the urge to do so. This may be with church staff, with friends in the program, or with other companions outside the program.

7. When people share important aspects of their lives, they can be assured that those things will be held in confidence by the rest of the group members.

The Unending Conversation

Imagine that you enter a parlor. You come late. When you arrive, others have long preceded you, and they are engaged in a heated discussion, a discussion too heated for them to pause and tell you exactly what it is about. In fact, the discussion had already begun long before any of them got there, so that no one present is qualified to retrace for you all the steps that had gone before. You listen for a while; then you put in your oar. Someone answers; you answer him; another comes to your defense; another aligns herself against you, to either the embarrassment or gratification of your opponent, depending upon the quality of your ally's assistance. However the discussion is interminable. The hour grows late, you must depart. And you do depart, with the discussion still vigorously in progress.*

Such is the "unending conversation" that has been going on since the beginning of human history and that we join at the moment of our birth and leave at the moment of our death.

Our task during these sessions together is

to continue to participate in the "unending conversation" of Christian theology

receiving
what we have been given within the tradition:
Bible, God, Jesus, Creeds, practice, and so on

interpreting
the received tradition
in our present cultural context, and

allowing
that which is "given" to have its own voice
in a changed cultural context.

*Kenneth Burke, *The Philosophy of Literary Form*, 3rd ed. (Berkeley: University of California Press, 1973; originally published in 1941, pp. 110–11.) Quoted by Marcus J. Borg in *The Heart of Christianity* (San Francisco: HarperSanFrancisco, 2003), pp. 19–20.

Two Paradigms: A Tale of Two Christianities...

	EARLIER CHRISTIANITY	EMERGING CHRISTIANITY
The Bible's Origin	*A divine product with divine authority.* The Bible comes from God as no other book does. The unique revelation of God. A divine product coming with a divine guarantee. The Bible is true because it comes from God.	*A human response to God.* The Bible was written for the ancient communities that produced it.
Biblical Interpretation	*Literal-factual.* Truth and factuality go hand in hand. "The miraculous" is central to the truth of Christianity.	*Historical and metaphorical.* It is more than literal and more than factual. Concerned with the meaning it has for us.
The Bible's Function	*Revelation of doctrine and morals.* The Bible as the revealed will of God is the ultimate authority for both faith and morals.	*Metaphorical and sacramental.* Sacred in its status and function, but not in its origin. Living within Bible and tradition as a means whereby the Spirit speaks to us.
Christian Life Emphasis	*Emphasis on an afterlife and what to believe or do to be saved.* It takes faith to believe things that are hard to believe. Really important question: where will you spend eternity? A religion of requirements and rewards. Believe in Christianity now for the sake of salvation later.	*Transformation in this life through relationship with God.* To be Christian does not mean believing in Christianity, but a relationship with God lived within the Christian metaphor and sacrament of the sacred.

Marcus J. Borg, *The Heart of Christianity* (San Francisco: HarperSanFrancisco, 2003), an expansion of the diagram presented on page 15 from the text of chapter 1.

The Prayer of Jesus

A paraphrase

Eternal Spirit,
Earth-maker, Pain-bearer, Life-giver,
Source of all that is and that shall be.
Father and Mother of us all,
Loving God, in whom is heaven:

The hallowing of your name echo through the universe!
The way of your justice be followed by peoples of the world!
Your heavenly will be done by all created beings!
Your commonwealth of peace and freedom sustain our hope
    and come on earth.

With the bread we need for today, feed us.
In the hurts we absorb from one another, forgive us.
In times of temptation and test, strengthen us.
From trials too great to endure, spare us.
From the grip of all that is evil, free us.

For you reign in the glory of the power that is love,
    now and forever.
Amen.

– Jim Cotter, 1988. Used by permission.

SESSION

2

FAITH: THE WAY OF THE HEART

INTEND

(This is for your guidance: you can share aspects of it with the group at any time that seems right to you.)

Outcomes for this session include the following:
- ❏ continuing to get to know one another;
- ❏ ensuring that people who did not attend the first session are included and that they receive handouts they missed in the first session;
- ❏ beginning to live into the purpose and principles of the program, as presented in the first session;
- ❏ hearing a story of faith from scripture that can illuminate our own faith exploration;
- ❏ beginning to share our own stories of faith;
- ❏ continuing to practice listening to one another, with openness and compassion;
- ❏ engaging with some of the ideas that Borg is presenting in this second chapter;
- ❏ using a variety of group configurations for conversation;
- ❏ confronting the reality of change;
- ❏ experiencing of the way of the heart;
- ❏ discovering that faith is about beloving God and all that God beloves.

PREPARE

☐ Familiarize yourself with Borg's four definitions of faith so that when you are receiving words from the group for each one and noting these on newsprint you will feel sufficiently conversant with his definition. Some key words are noted in "Engage 2."

☐ Post the "Welcome" page for people to see as they arrive.

☐ Place water and drinking glasses on a side table that is easily accessible to all.

☐ Choose a circular place for the group's "Pilgrim Walk." This might be in the sanctuary, somewhere in the grounds of the church, in a hall, or in a home or garden. A lot depends on where you meet and what space is available. Basically, you need a circle large enough to accommodate all members of the group walking at the same time, with good spacing between them. Make signs with the names of the months of the year that can be placed on the floor equidistant around the circle.

☐ Place a candle on a central table; have matches ready.

☐ You will need newsprint and markers for a couple of processes.

☐ Make copies of "Hebrews 11:8–16, adapted" (page 56).

☐ Make extra copies of the paraphrase of "The Prayer of Jesus," which was used in the previous session (page 45).

☐ Prepare a half-page handout describing what people are to bring for Session 3, which will focus on the Bible. See the "Anticipate" section of this session.

WELCOME

Make sure the following words of welcome and instruction are written on newsprint and displayed in a spot where everyone can read them as they arrive:

Welcome to Session 2, Faith: The Way of the Heart
As you wait for the session to begin, please sit with someone new to you and talk together about what it's like for you to live in times of fast-paced change.

OPEN

The passage of scripture used in the opening is available as a handout so that people can participate in the reading.

Welcome to this next stage of our journey of exploration and learning. Over the next four weeks, we will be seeing the Christian *tradition* again, looking particularly at faith, the Bible, God, and Jesus. In the remaining sessions after that, we will be seeing the Christian *life* again.

As with any journey, there is uncertainty and there is mystery, there is anxiety and there is excitement.

Change is inevitable.

Resisting change expends energy that could be given to living with the new emerging thing.

Here is light for your journey into the unknown of God's future. (Light the candle.)

Here is water to refresh you as you go with your companions. (Indicate the water.)

Share and drink, as you need to.

Here are sacred words from our own tradition: a remembrance of a man and a woman who, thousands of years ago, also went on a journey of faith, a journey of the heart.

Hebrews 11:8–16 (adapted)

By faith Abraham and Sarah obeyed when they were called to set out for a place that they were to receive as an inheritance;

and they set out, not knowing where they were going.

By faith they stayed for a time in the land they had been promised, as in a foreign land, living in tents, as did their children, who were heirs with them of the same promise.

For they looked forward to the city that has foundations, whose architect and builder is God.

By faith they received power of procreation, even though they were too old – and Sarah herself was barren – because they considered faithful the one who had promised.

Therefore from these people, as good as dead, descendants were born, "as many as the stars of heaven and as the innumerable grains of sand by the seashore."

Many died in faith without having received the promises, but from a distance they saw and greeted them.

They confessed that they were strangers and foreigners on the earth, for people who speak in this way make it clear that they are seeking a homeland.

If they had been thinking of the land that they had left behind, they would have had opportunity to return.

But as it is, they desire a better country, that is, a heavenly one.

Therefore God is not ashamed to be called their God; indeed, God has prepared a city for them.

As we gather here again, let's also name ourselves people of faith, people on a road not knowing where we are going, people of whom it could be said, "God is not ashamed to be called their God." We will go around the circle; each person will say their name and everyone else will respond by repeating that name.

CONNECT

Group check-in. (This might be in groups of four, if you have more than 12 participants. If you have fewer than 12, then check in around the circle.)

We will take time now to talk about where our journeys of faith have taken us since we were together last time. For those of you who were here for the first session, this might include some reflection on what transpired as a result of that session. If you were not here last time, listen in, and, as your turn comes, speak about what attracted you to this program.

ENGAGE

(Option: If you collated and printed the questions that were recorded last week, this would be a good time to hand them out to group members. They provide a way of tracking the issues of concern for the group in its first session and of empowering people to find their own responses as they go through each session.)

Engage 1: Continuums

Last week's chapter was entitled "The Heart of Christianity in a Time of Change." For some of us, what Marcus Borg describes as "emerging" Christianity may call for a lot of change. We may feel that we are closer to what he calls "earlier" Christianity. What all of us may actually have most in common is a sense that we are going to emerge from this course changed somehow.

In this session, we will focus intentionally on the question of change and think about the place of change in our own faith and spiritual journeys. An efficient way to have this kind of conversation is to put ourselves on a line called a continuum. Let's try it.

Imagine a line running through the room from here to here. At one end is one response to the topic I give; at the other end, the opposite response. In between there may be degrees of response. I

will invite you to stand on the line at the place that feels most right to you. There will be four continuums. Here's the first one:

CONTINUUM 1

As you think about changes in matters of faith of the magnitude that Borg is proposing, what feelings are typical for you?

1			10
fearfulness/ avoidance of change at all costs	anxiety/change only when necessary	somewhat neutral/ change is necessary; I can deal with it	bring on the change!/ change and life are inseparable

Talk with someone near you about why you chose to stand where you did. What feelings do you most experience in regard to significant change? (Record some of these on newsprint when people have had time for their conversation.)

Now here's the next continuum:

CONTINUUM 2

As you think about your own faith journey since childhood, would you say…

1		10
I have changed very little in matters of faith	I have changed somewhat in matters of faith	I am hardly recognizable as the same person

Talk with someone near you about why you chose to stand where you did. What kinds of changes have you experienced?

Now the third continuum:

CONTINUUM 3

As you begin to get a sense of the ideas that Borg is presenting, how far do you see him from where you are?

1		10
Far, far away from me	Some similarities	Quite close

As you are all standing on the line, tell the group what makes you think this is where you should be standing.

CONTINUUM 4

There are only going to be two points on this line – one at each end. Choose a number between 1 and 10 to represent where you would be in relation to these two different approaches to the Christian faith:

1	10
The Way of Right Belief Believing a set of statements to be true Affirming the "right" set of beliefs matters (beliefs about biblical teaching, doctrines, and dogma) Faith primarily a matter of beliefs	**The Way of the Heart** Three affirmations are foundational: the reality of God, the centrality of Jesus, the centrality of the Bible. Other than that, the Christian life is about loving God and all that God loves. Faith is our love for God.

Find someone at a different place on the continuum than you and share with one another why you stood where you did.

Engage 2: The Four Meanings of Faith
In this chapter, Borg defines the meaning of faith in four different ways. I've divided this newsprint page into four quadrants, one for each of these definitions. Rather than reading his descriptions again, let's try to find words together to represent each meaning. These may be your words as much as Borg's.

Fiducia
The kind of words people may offer: radical trust in God – trusting in the buoyancy of God – God, the one on whom we rely, our safe place – as trust grows, anxiety diminishes.

Fidelitas
The kind of words people may offer: faithfulness – radical centering in God – being attentive to relationship with God in prayer and practice – loving God and loving that which God loves.

Visio
The kind of words people may offer: a way of seeing that shapes our relationship to "what is" – seeing the whole as either hostile and threatening, indifferent, or life-giving and nourishing.

Assensus
The kind of words people may offer: assent to a proposition – a "head" matter – believing in the right things – believing even when there is reason to think otherwise.

In the time of reflection that follows, you might keep people in the total group or, if the group is larger than 12, break up into groups of three or four.

Let's talk together about two things:

1. the "meaning of faith" that has particular appeal at this time in our lives,
2. the relationship between change and faith.

Engage 3: A Pilgrim Walk: The Way of the Heart

In his closing statement in this chapter, Borg says, "Faith is about beloving God and all that God beloves. The Christian life is about beloving God and all that God beloves. Faith is our love for God. Faith is the way of the heart."

We live relationship with this loving God a year at a time. As you move through a year, your relationship with God takes on different qualities reflecting your journey through the year. Pilgrims, such as you and I, have frequently gone on pilgrimages of faith and when they couldn't do that, they have walked paths within their sanctuaries; paths sometimes shaped like labyrinths. We are going to walk the cycle of a year right now, in this circular space I have prepared. You will find the names of the months marked equidistant from each other. As you walk through each month, reflect on your relationship with this beloving and beloved God in that month of the year.

When you have finished, take time to reflect by yourself on the significance of your walk. You might make notes in your journal. When you are ready, move into a group of three or four and talk together about what you experienced in the Pilgrim Walk.

ANTICIPATE

In preparation for next week when our focus is on the Bible, please do two things:

1. Choose a favorite character from the Bible, whom you will name when you introduce yourself to the group next week.
2. Choose and bring with you a passage of scripture through which the Spirit has spoken to you in some way at some time in your life.

CLOSE

By faith Abraham and Sarah obeyed when they were called to set out for a place that they were to receive as an inheritance; and they set out, not knowing where they were going. As you set out from here this week, do so in the assurance that you are accompanied by the presence of God who is known in the lives and voices of this community. Let us say the Prayer of Jesus as we prepare to leave.

Hebrews 11:8–16 (adapted)

By faith Abraham and Sarah obeyed when they were called to set out for a place that they were to receive as an inheritance;

and they set out, not knowing where they were going.

By faith they stayed for a time in the land they had been promised, as in a foreign land, living in tents, as did their children, who were heirs with them of the same promise.

For they looked forward to the city that has foundations, whose architect and builder is God.

By faith they received power of procreation, even though they were too old – and Sarah herself was barren – because they considered faithful the one who had promised.

Therefore from these people, as good as dead, descendants were born, "as many as the stars of heaven and as the innumerable grains of sand by the seashore."

Many died in faith without having received the promises, but from a distance they saw and greeted them.

They confessed that they were strangers and foreigners on the earth, for people who speak in this way make it clear that they are seeking a homeland.

If they had been thinking of the land that they had left behind, they would have had opportunity to return.

But as it is, they desire a better country, that is, a heavenly one.

Therefore God is not ashamed to be called their God; indeed, God has prepared a city for them.

SESSION

3

THE BIBLE:
THE HEART OF THE TRADITION

INTEND

(This is for your guidance: you can share aspects of it with the group at any time that seems right to you.)

Outcomes for this session include the following:

❏ being guided in and enriched by connecting personal life and social context to the Bible;

❏ continuing to build lifelong relationship with God, who is disclosed to us in the Bible, which can be both metaphor and sacrament to us;

❏ reflecting on the place that scripture has occupied and continues to occupy in our lives;

❏ engaging with Borg's emphasis on the centrality of the Bible in Christian life.

PREPARE

❏ Place water and drinking glasses on a side table that is easily accessible to all.

❏ Post the "Welcome" page for people to see as they arrive.

❏ Place a candle on a central table; have matches ready.

❏ Have a Bible ready to place on the table beside the candle.

❏ Have extra copies of the paraphrase of "The Prayer of Jesus," available (page 45).

❑ Make copies of the handout "A page to support participation in Session 3" (page 64).

❑ Make copies of "Biblical Bingo" and have them available for people as they arrive at the session (page 65).

❑ Have a DVD player and TV or data projector ready to play the Marcus Borg video clip, "A Metaphoric Approach to Scripture," under the "for groups" menu.

WELCOME

Make sure the following words of welcome and the instruction to play "Biblical Bingo" are written on newsprint and displayed in a spot where everyone can read them as they arrive:

Welcome to Session 3, The Bible: The Heart of the Tradition
Take one of the "Biblical Bingo" pages. Find people who "fit" each square on the page. Note their names in the spaces provided.

OPEN

The "Biblical Bingo" game is really a feature both of opening and connecting, so you can let the activity proceed until people have filled in a couple of lines on their cards and visited with a number of people. This will give people who arrive right on time opportunity to participate in the activity. There will be a chance to check in later in the process.

Welcome to this time, in a community of story-makers and storytellers. I light this candle as a reminder of God's presence with us here in this community. (Light the candle.)
People desiring to know God more fully have, for many, many centuries shared light as a sign of Holy presence.
Today I place a Bible, our sacred text, here beside the candle.
May the Bible be for us, too, a source of illumination in our desire to be ever more fully God's people.

In the Psalms we read these words:

God visits the earth and waters it.

God turns a desert into pools of water, a parched land into springs of water.

The river of God is full of water.

God waters the furrows abundantly, softening the earth with showers, and blessing its growth.

The water of God is here for you in abundance; drink as you feel thirsty.

The water of life is here for you as we share our lives together in community.

May we know the comfort and challenge of God's Spirit among us as we spend this time together. May it be so.

CONNECT

As we come together in this circle of learning, let's again hear one another's names. Let's also hear the name of a biblical character that is a favorite of yours. You might also like to say briefly what attracts you to that character.

Go around the circle and hear people's names and biblical characters, as people are ready to share.

The "Biblical Bingo" page was intended as a way for you to think about some of the places the Bible occupies in our lives and in our stories. It was also a way for you to meet others, as we gathered here for this session. We will do two more things with the Biblical Bingo page:

1. See if we can name together the fruits that are commonly mentioned in the Bible (grapes, olives, figs, dates, apples and pomegranates).

2. Name insights you have from hearing others talking about the place the Bible occupied in their lives.

ENGAGE

In this chapter, Marcus Borg emphasizes the power of the Bible to be both metaphor and sacrament in our lives. Our time in this session will be given to experiencing those two things.

Engage 1: Bible as Metaphor

We will use a simple verbal structure to practice seeing metaphorically through Bible story:

When I hear the story of _____,
I see my life with God in this way: _____.

Let's practice this together using a common story from the Christian tradition. Hear the story, which is printed for you on the handout "A Page to Support Participation in Session 3."

Luke 8:22–25

One day he got into a boat with his disciples, and he said to them, "Let us go across to the other side of the lake." So they put out, and while they were sailing he fell asleep. A windstorm swept down on the lake, and the boat was filling with water, and they were in danger. They went to him and woke him up, shouting, "Master, Master, we are perishing!" And he woke up and rebuked the wind and the raging waves; they ceased, and there was a calm. He said to them, "Where is your faith?" They were afraid and amazed, and said to one another, "Who then is this, that he commands even the winds and the water, and they obey him?"

Hear the story once again.

Now take a few minutes on your own to ask yourself how this brief story opens one window on how you see your relationship with God. Complete the following statement, which you will find on the handout right after the passage of scripture:

When I hear the story of Jesus calming the storm,
I see my life with God in this way: _____.

1. After people have had time to write their response, call the group together to hear people's responses. The size of your group will determine whether you stay in the total group or move into groups of three or four for this discussion.
2. After hearing people's responses to the story, provide time in the total group to talk about this "metaphoric" approach to scripture. If you have access to a DVD player and TV or data projector, then play the Marcus Borg clip, "A Metaphoric Approach to Scripture." This will enrich the group discussion. Monitor your time so that you still have enough time to focus on the Bible as sacrament.

Engage 2: Bible as Sacrament
At this time, we will experience the Bible as sacrament. You will have an opportunity to bring to the group a passage of scripture through which the Spirit has spoken to you in some way – a passage of scripture through which you have been particularly aware of God's accompanying presence.

We will take five minutes in silence while you make sure you have the passage that feels like the right one for this process. (Spend five minutes in silence.)

The size of your group will determine whether you stay in the total group or move into groups of three or four for this discussion. If you have eight or more people in the group, it would be advisable to be in smaller groups, because of the time it takes to hear and to respond.

The following instructions are printed on the handout, "A Page to Support Participation in Session 3."

Each person will bring their scripture passage to the group in this way:

1. Read the passage aloud while the others listen.
2. Speak about the way that God (Spirit, the "More") has been present to you through this passage.
3. Invite other members of the group to speak about the impact the passage had on them, as they heard it in this session or as they have experienced it before.
4. Respond with any new insights you have as a result of hearing from others.
5. Close by reading the passage aloud again.

After everyone has had an opportunity to present their scripture passage in this way, provide time in the total group to talk about this "sacramental" approach to scripture. This will probably lead into a conversation about Marcus Borg's teaching on the topic of the Bible as sacrament. Monitor your time so that you have an opportunity to bring the whole session to a close with a reading and a prayer.

ANTICIPATE

As you go through the time between this session and the next, carry with you the instructions offered by Marcus Borg on page 73, when he quotes these words of Frederick Buechner. You will find these instructions at the bottom of the page, "A Page to Support Participation in Session 3."

"Listen to your life. Listen to what happens to you because it is through what happens to you that God speaks. It's in language that's not always easy to decipher, but it's there powerfully, memorably, unforgettably."

CLOSE

Affirmation:

God visits the earth and waters it.

God turns a desert into pools of water, a parched land into springs of
water.

The river of God is full of water.

God waters the furrows abundantly, softening the earth with showers,
and blessing its growth.

Christ sails with us to the other side.

Christ turns a raging storm into calm waters, a place of terror into
amazement.

The sea of Christ is full of possibility.

Christ rebukes the wind, softening the storm with authority, and
accompanying our way.

**As we come to the end of this time, we will say again the paraphrase
of the Prayer of Jesus. Let us pray together.**

A Page to Support Participation in Session 3
The Bible: The Heart of the Christian Tradition

Engage 1: Bible as Metaphor

The Story: Luke 8:22–25
One day he got into a boat with his disciples,
and he said to them, "Let us go across to the other side of the lake."

So they put out, and while they were sailing he fell asleep.
A windstorm swept down on the lake, and the boat was filling with water,
and they were in danger.

They went to him and woke him up, shouting, "Master, Master, we are perishing!"
And he woke up and rebuked the wind and the raging waves; they ceased,
and there was a calm.

He said to them, "Where is your faith?"
They were afraid and amazed,
and said to one another,
"Who then is this, that he commands even the winds and the water, and they obey him?"

When I hear the story of Jesus calming the storm, I see my life with God in this way:

_____

Engage 2: Bible as Sacrament

Each person takes a turn bringing their scripture passage to the group in this way:
1. Read the passage aloud while the others listen.
2. Speak about the way that God (Spirit, the "More") has been present to you through this passage.
3. Invite other members of the group to speak about the impact the passage had on them as they heard it in this session or as they have experienced it before.
4. Respond with any new insights you have as a result of hearing from others.
5. Close by reading the passage again aloud.

Preparation for Next Week
As you go through the time between this session and the next, carry with you the instructions offered by Marcus Borg on page 73, when he quotes these words of Frederick Buechner:

> *"Listen to your life. Listen to what happens to you because it is through what happens to you that God speaks. It's in language that's not always easy to decipher, but it's there powerfully, memorably, unforgettably."*

Biblical Bingo

FIND SOMEONE...

...who had a grandparent who read Bible stories to them when they were a child. (Do they recall any story in particular?) Name:_____	...who still has a Bible from their childhood. (What do they remember about it?) Name:_____	...who has a name taken from the Bible. (Who chose it for them?) Name:_____	...who has traveled to a place mentioned in the Bible. (What did they see there?) Name:_____
...who has seen and appreciated at least one film based on a biblical story. (What did they like about it?) Name:_____	...who memorized some verses from the Bible. (Do they still know them?) Name:_____	...who has a specific preference for one Bible translation over others. (Why do they have that preference?) Name:_____	...who is intentional about passing on Bible stories to a younger generation. (How do they do that?) Name:_____
...who knows exactly how many Bibles they have in their home. (Do they also remember where they all are?) Name:_____	...who has used the Bible for some purpose other than the one intended. (What was that use?) Name:_____	...who knows how to say "Bible" in another language. (How did they come to know that?) Name:_____	...who has heard a rabbi teaching the Torah, God's instruction to Israel based on the Hebrew Scriptures. (How did that come about?) Name:_____
...who has performed in a biblical drama of some kind. (What part did they play?) Name:_____	...who has eaten at least three fruits that are mentioned in the Bible. (What are they?) Name:_____	...who feels confident to find any book of the Bible. (What method do they use?) Name:_____	...who sometimes makes reference in conversation to Bible stories and characters. (Can they name one of those references?) Name:_____

SESSION

4

——

GOD: THE HEART OF REALITY

INTEND

(This is for your guidance: you can share aspects of it with the group at any
time that seems right to you.)

Outcomes for this session include the following:
- ❏ continuing to build a community of trust where it is possible to
  share those things that matter most;
- ❏ being challenged to think about what we mean by "God";
- ❏ speaking about and experiencing together that encompassing
  Spirit that is the very ground of our being, the one in whom "we
  live and move and have our being";
- ❏ seeing how we shape our experience of God through the hymns we
  sing;
- ❏ engaging in a ritual of giving God's blessing to one another.

PREPARE
- ❏ Place water and drinking glasses on a side table that is easily
  accessible to all.
- ❏ Post the "Welcome" page for people to see as they arrive.
- ❏ Place a candle on a central table; have matches ready.
- ❏ Write on newsprint the names for God to which you will refer after
  reading Psalm 139: Companion of the Way, Seeker and Finder,
  Spirit Presence, Morning Wings, Night Light, Source of Wonder,
  Frame Weaver, Still with Me.

❑   You will need newsprint for another part of the process.

❑   Choose four or five hymns from your hymnal, or from other
sources, that address the reality of God in some way. If you
are able to have someone present to accompany the group
in singing the hymns, then make those arrangements. These
are five hymns I chose from the United Church of Canada's
hymnbook *Voices United:*

VU#268	*Bring Many Names*
VU#282	*Long Before the Night*
VU#229	*God of the Sparrow*
VU#265	*Creating God, Your Fingers Trace*
VU#278	*In the Quiet Curve of Evening*

You might decide not to choose hymns ahead of time, but to wait
until the session and let the members of the group choose the
hymns they like.

❑   Prepare copies of the three handouts: "A Page to Support
Participation in Session 4 – God: The Heart of Reality," "Psalm
139:1–14," and "Frames of Comparison Presented by Marcus
Borg in Chapter 4" (pages 74–76)

❑   Have extra copies of the paraphrase of "The Prayer of Jesus,"
available (page 45).

WELCOME

Make sure the following words of welcome and the instructions to
"check in" are written on newsprint and displayed in a spot where
everyone can read them as they arrive:

Welcome to Session 4, God: The Heart of Reality
Check in with someone with whom you haven't spent much time in previous
sessions.

OPEN

Before you begin the opening, hand out copies of these two pages: "Psalm 139:1–14," and "A Page to Support Participation in Session 4."

What a gift to come into a community of companion-seekers ready to bring our hearts and minds together *to wonder about* the very ground and heart of reality!

- **Let us open our minds and hearts *to wonder* about the kinds of ideas that Marcus Borg so clearly articulates in this chapter.**
- **Let us open ourselves – body, mind, and spirit – to be *in wonder* at all that is both mysterious and revealed in the reality we refer to as God.**

God's gifts to us are more numerous than the sand of the seashore.
Here is the gift of light for our journey. (Light the candle.)
Here is the gift of water for your refreshment. (Pour the water into the bowl.)

As we sit in the presence of the light, the water, and the community, let us read together the first 14 verses from an ancient text, a poem and a song about the intimacy of God: Psalm 139. We will all read the opening and closing lines together, and go around the circle hearing one another read the other verses.

Psalm 139:1–14
All: O God, you have searched me and known me.

You know when I sit down and when I rise up; you discern my thoughts from far away.

You search out my path and my lying down, and are acquainted with all my ways.

Even before a word is on my tongue, O God, you know it completely.

You hem me in, behind and before, and lay your hand upon me.

Such knowledge is too wonderful for me; it is so high that I cannot attain it.

Where can I go from your spirit? Or where can I flee from your presence?

If I ascend to heaven, you are there; if I make my bed in Sheol, you are there.

If I take the wings of the morning and settle at the farthest limits of the sea, even there your hand shall lead me, and your right hand shall hold me fast.

If I say, "Surely the darkness shall cover me, and the light around me become night," even the darkness is not dark to you; the night is as bright as the day, for darkness is as light to you.

For it was you who formed my inward parts; you knit me together in my mother's womb.

I praise you, for I am fearfully and wonderfully made.

All: Wonderful are your works; that I know very well.

In chapter 4 of the book, Marcus Borg affirms that we each have a personal relationship with God, a relationship that "engages us at our deepest and most passionate level." A relationship of that kind often includes the choice of names for the other one in the relationship, names based on qualities of character that become evident in the intimacy of relationship.

Imagine if the poet of Psalm 139 had chosen names for God. The list might have included these names (on newsprint):

- **Companion of the Way**
- **Seeker and Finder**
- **Spirit Presence**
- **Morning Wings**
- **Night Light**
- **Source of Wonder**
- **Frame Weaver**
- **Still with Me**

What are our names for God on this day? As we sit together at the beginning of this session, let's call out names for God that have meaning for us, recognizing that some names last for a long time, and others suit one day and not the next. Feel free to call out the names you have for God right at this moment, as well as names that come from the story of your relationship with God.

(Record the names that people call out on newsprint. Later in the process of the session there will be an opportunity to add to the list. Invite people to add to the list as the session progresses and as names for God come into their awareness.)

We will sit here speaking and hearing these names for as long as we need.

Say prayer after speaking the names of God (on the "Participation" handout).

Let us all pray together:

O God, you have searched us and known us;

be the light of our discerning,

be the wings of our imagining,

be the worker of our wonder,

be the breath of our conversation,

be the ground of our journey,

now and forever. Amen.

CONNECT

The size of your group will determine whether you stay in the total group or move into groups of three or four for this discussion.

We return now to the quote from author Frederick Buechner, on page 73 of *The Heart of Christianity*. This is the quote I gave you last session as a way to reflect on your relationship with God. Before we begin our discussion, we should note Borg's caution in the paragraph following not to interpret this as meaning that everything that happens is the direct will of God.

"Listen to your life. Listen to what happens to you because it is through what happens to you that God speaks. It's in language that's not always easy to decipher, but it's there powerfully, memorably, unforgettably."

Now we will speak together about experiences where you have listened to your life and heard God speaking. (If people are in small groups, let them know how long they have for this time of sharing and encourage them to share the time equally among the group members.)

ENGAGE

Engage 1: Three Frames of Comparison from Chapter 4

The size of your group will determine whether you stay in the total group or move into groups of three or four for this discussion.

Hand out the page "Frames of Comparison Presented by Marcus Borg in Chapter 4."

You've read this chapter so you have experienced Marcus Borg's careful progression through some ways of thinking of God. This handout is a brief summary of some of Borg's presentation. It is intended as a prompt for the conversations we are about to have.

You will have three conversations, each one seven minutes in length. There is a leading question for each conversation.

Conversation 1: Worldviews

Question: What experiences have you had, or what data do you possess, that persuade you toward the religious or non-religious worldview?

Conversation 2: Concepts of God

Question: What descriptive words have meaning and power for you as you think about your concept of God?

Conversation 3: The Character of God

Question: On a continuum from 1–10 between these two extremes that describe the character of God, where would you put yourself? How has this changed during your lifetime?

Engage 2: Hymns of God

In our tradition we sing our faith in community. Our hymns contribute to our worship of God. When we sing hymns, we sing our theology; we put what we believe about God into our mouths and into our beings. Let's sing some hymns together and discuss what beliefs about God are reflected in these popular hymns.

After singing each hymn, ask questions such as these:

- **What is the impact of this hymn on you?**
- **What does the hymn writer seem to be saying about God in this hymn?**
- **In what ways does this match your experience of God?**
- **Are there some names for God suggested by this hymn that we could add to our list?**
- **What difference does it make in your relationship with God to sing hymns in community?**

ANTICIPATE

Take the passage from Isaiah that we will be using shortly in our closing for this session. Post it somewhere in your home, where you will be reminded of it. Say it aloud, inserting your name in the blank spaces. Take time to reflect on the power of its message for your life right now.

CLOSE

This blessing ritual takes a couple of minutes for each person. If you have time and your total group is 12 or less, you might consider doing it with everyone together. Otherwise do it in groups of 4 to 6 people. It can be very powerful; there is merit in having everyone experience it together.

In our closing time this evening, we are going to participate in a ritual of blessing one another. Let's all stand in a circle. In turn, each of you will come into the center of the circle. The rest of the group members will read this passage from Isaiah, inserting the person's name in the blank spaces.

But now thus says God who created you, _____,
God who formed you _____:
Do not fear, for I have redeemed you;
I have called you by name, _____, you are mine.
When you pass through the waters, I will be with you;
and through the rivers, they shall not overwhelm you;
when you walk through the fire you shall not be burned,
and the flame shall not consume you.
For I am your God.

Isaiah 43:1–3a

As we come to the end of this time of learning in community, we will say again the paraphrase of the Prayer of Jesus. Let us pray together.

Frames of Comparison
Presented by Marcus Borg in Chapter 4 – "God: The Heart of Reality"

WORLDVIEWS

Religious Worldview
- There is "MORE" than the visible world
- There is a nonmaterial layer or level of reality named as God, Spirit, the sacred, Yahweh, the Tao, Allah, Brahman, Atman, and so on
- Data: witness and wisdom of world's religions, sacred religious and visionary experiences, affirmations of post-modern science

Non-religious Worldview
- There is no "MORE"; there is only "This"
- There is only a world of matter and energy
- The universe is giant system of particles plus force fields operating within natural laws

CONCEPTS OF GOD

Supernatural Theism
- God, as a person-like supreme being, created the world separate from God
- God is "up in heaven" or "out there"
- God occasionally "intervenes" in world
- This intervention may include spectacular events
- God continues to intervene, especially in response to prayer
- God is more remote as universe grows

Panentheism
- God as encompassing Spirit in whom everything that is, is
- the universe is in God, not separate from God
- God is the one in whom "we live and move and have our being" (Paul)
- God is "right here" and "more than right here"
- God transcendent (the More) and God immanent (right here)
- not God of intervention, but God of intention and interaction

THE CHARACTER OF GOD

It makes a difference how we see the character of God, for how we see the character of God shapes our sense of what faithfulness to God means and thus what the Christian life is about. – Marcus Borg

God of Requirements & Rewards
God of Law
- God as lawgiver and judge
- "The monarchical model of God"
- Relationship is expressed in legal language: our disobedience – Jesus' sacrifice – salvation
- If you believe you will be saved

God of Love & Justice / God of Grace
- The language of love speaks of God's relationship with Israel
- God of love is God of justice (in Bible justice is the social form of love)
- God loves everybody and everything
- The Christian life is about a relationship with God that transforms us into more compassionate people

A Page to Support Participation in Session 4
God: The Heart of Reality

Prayer after speaking the names of God

> O God, you have searched us and known us;
> be the light of our discerning,
> be the wings of our imagining,
> be the worker of our wonder,
> be the breath of our conversation,
> be the ground of our journey,
> now and forever. Amen.

Quote from Frederick Buechner, page 73 of the text

> *"Listen to your life. Listen to what happens to you because it is through what happens to you that God speaks. It's in language that's not always easy to decipher, but it's there powerfully, memorably, unforgettably."*

Guide for Conversations in Engage 1

Conversation 1: Worldviews

Question: What experiences have you had, or what data do you possess, that persuade you toward the religious or non-religious worldview?

Conversation 2: Concepts of God

Question: What descriptive words have meaning and power for you as you think about your concept of God?

Conversation 3: The Character of God

Question: On a continuum from 1–10 between these two extremes that describe the character of God, where would you put yourself? How has this changed during your lifetime?

Isaiah Blessing Ritual for Closing and for the Week Ahead

> But now thus says God who created you, _____,
> God who formed you _____:
> Do not fear, for I have redeemed you;
> I have called you by name, _____, you are mine.
> When you pass through the waters, I will be with you;
> and through the rivers, they shall not overwhelm you;
> when you walk through the fire you shall not be burned,
> and the flame shall not consume you.
> For I am your God.
>
> *– Isaiah 43:1-3a*

Psalm 139:1–14

All: O God, you have searched me and known me.

- You know when I sit down and when I rise up; you discern my thoughts from far away.

- You search out my path and my lying down, and are acquainted with all my ways.

- Even before a word is on my tongue, O God, you know it completely.

- You hem me in, behind and before, and lay your hand upon me.

- Such knowledge is too wonderful for me; it is so high that I cannot attain it.

- Where can I go from your spirit? Or where can I flee from your presence?

- If I ascend to heaven, you are there; if I make my bed in Sheol, you are there.

- If I take the wings of the morning and settle at the farthest limits of the sea, even there your hand shall lead me, and your right hand shall hold me fast.

- If I say, "Surely the darkness shall cover me, and the light around me become night," even the darkness is not dark to you; the night is as bright as the day, for darkness is as light to you.

- For it was you who formed my inward parts; you knit me together in my mother's womb.

- I praise you, for I am fearfully and wonderfully made.

All: Wonderful are your works; that I know very well.

SESSION

5

___

JESUS: THE HEART OF GOD

INTEND

(This is for your guidance: you can share aspects of it with the group at any time that seems right to you.)

Outcomes for this session include the following:

❏ providing a setting in which each participant will feel encouraged to answer the question, "Who is Jesus for you?";

❏ hearing the reported words of Jesus to draw us into the drama of his living;

❏ looking at artistic images of Jesus to stimulate our own reflection on who he is for us;

❏ recalling the place of Jesus in our lives;

❏ being stretched by Marcus Borg in our consideration of who Jesus is for us today;

❏ writing imaginatively in response to the question of Jesus: "Who do you say that I am?";

❏ taking a historical, metaphorical, and sacramental approach to "seeing Jesus again";

❏ appreciating the uniqueness of this religion, which reveals God in a person.

PREPARE

❏ Place water and drinking glasses on a side table that is easily accessible to all.

❏ Post the "welcome" page for people to see as they arrive.

❏ Place a candle on a central table; have matches ready.

❏ Have extra copies of the paraphrase of "The Prayer of Jesus," available (page 45).

❏ Make copies of the four handouts for this session: "Words of Jesus," "Quotes from Chapter 5," "Ten Statements about Jesus that are True for Me," and "Alphapoem" (pages 86–89).

❏ Have a DVD player and TV or data projector ready to display the images of Jesus, included on the DVD, in Engage 1. If you do not have access to a DVD player, gather your own collection of images of Jesus to pass around the circle. You will also need to use the DVD player to show the Marcus Borg clip, "The Distinction Between 'Jesus' and 'Christ,'" under the "for groups" menu. You will be using this clip in Engage 2.

❏ Bring a bell (or some other pleasant percussive instrument) to ring during the exercise of passing the images of Jesus.

WELCOME

Make sure the following words of welcome are written on newsprint and displayed in a spot where everyone can read them as they arrive:

Welcome to Session 5, Jesus: the Heart of God
The bread of community and the water of new life are here for you.

OPEN

Circulate the handout "Words of Jesus," which will be used during this opening time.

It is reported that Jesus said to his friends, "Come away to a deserted place all by yourselves and rest a while." There were undoubtedly many occasions on which Jesus invited his friends to come together, to gather in community.

As we gather here in this community of learning, there's a sense in which we too have been invited by Jesus to "come away":

come away to be together in a community of discernment;

come away to converse together about matters that are of deepest consequence to us;

come away to answer a question that Jesus himself asked of his friends, "Who do people say that I am?"

The candle is lit.

As we light the candle, let us hear the challenge of Jesus, who still asks the question, "Is a lamp brought in to be put under the bushel basket, or under the bed, and not on the lamp stand? For there is nothing hidden, except to be disclosed; nor is anything secret, except to come to light."

May this light call us into a place of trust and compassion, where things may be brought to light so that we may learn and be changed.

Some of the words of Jesus are recorded in scripture. As we begin this session, let's allow some of these words to enter us and to call us into the larger story of his life, which is both recorded and unrecorded.

You will find these words on the handout "Words of Jesus." We will keep reading around our circle until we come to the end of the statements. Don't rush in your reading. Let's read at a pace that allows the words to evoke images, stories, and meanings that we associate with these words of Jesus.

Read the words of Jesus.

Know this. As we spend this time together listening, searching, awakening, stretching, touching, and giving, there is a light in our midst that is clear and unhidden; there is water that is clear and for sharing.

CONNECT

Begin by sharing some opening reflections on this session's focus.

We have a tremendous amount of choice in this matter of Jesus; we are only as limited in exploring a new relationship with Jesus as we choose to be.

Inasmuch as that is true, it mirrors some of the truth of Jesus' life: don't be bound by the past; cast off the things that keep you imprisoned; look at all that's possible in this amazing creation God has birthed us to; open your eyes and see the systems that keep you confined, as they really are; learn to trust your own instincts and imagination.

Marcus Borg makes a strong case for the emerging paradigm's way of seeing Jesus, a way of seeing Jesus that is of an emerging paradigm, which is quite different from the Jesus of the earlier paradigm, who is still very attractive to many Christians. We will be influenced by Borg's writing and teaching, but ultimately we each have to affirm who Jesus is for us. We will continue that process this evening, not thinking that it will be complete, but that it will continue through the remaining sessions of this program.

We will begin our discussion process in paired conversations, changing partners after the first conversation.

Conversation 1:
Talk together about the ways you thought of Jesus when you were a child (perhaps making reference to one of your childhood experiences of Jesus).

Conversation 2:
Talk together about the characteristics of Jesus that really appeal to you as an adult today.

At the end of this conversation, have people call out some of the characteristics they named. You might record these on newsprint as they are called out, so that people can respond to them after the list is finished. Allow time for people to respond to the list, acknowledging that they may not be comfortable with all the words on it, and that it might contain words they might not have thought of themselves, but that they would now choose.

Here are some examples from another group: Compassionate, rebellious, feisty, passionate, kind, creative, inclusive, healer, gentle, strong, challenging, accepting, prayerful, believer, political, angry, unforgettable, courageous, peaceful, insightful, humble, loving, comforting and discomforting, beautiful, human, mystical, generous, curious, storyteller.

ENGAGE

Engage 1: Images of Jesus

In calling out the characteristics and qualities of Jesus, you might have noticed images of his physical reality forming in your mind. These might have been completely original with you, or they might have been informed by artistic representations of Jesus that have been created over the centuries.

We are going to look at some of these highly imaginative artistic renderings of Jesus and allow our awareness of who Jesus was and is to expand. You will notice that these images are in a variety of styles, from a diversity of cultures and from different periods of history.

If you are viewing these pictures on a screen, take time for people to rearrange their chairs and get comfortable so that they are really able to be present to the procession of images. If you are using your own collection of images, then sit in a circle, close enough to pass the pictures from one to another.

You might choose to create a rhythm to the passing of the images by ringing the bell (or other percussive instrument) every 15 seconds, as a signal that it's time to pass the image to the next person.

As you receive (see) each image, look at it, noticing its impact on you.

When all the images have been viewed, show them a second time. As you do this, ask each person to identify the image that has the most impact on them, as it appears on the screen.

If you are using printed images, after the first viewing, either have people place them on their chairs or arrange them on a table where they can all be seen at one time. Offer people the following instruction.

Walk around revisiting the images and remembering the impact that each one had on you. Go to the image that had the most impact on you. What is it about that picture that draws you?

Take time for people to talk about their response to the images, both ones that attracted and ones that did not.

Engage 2: Ideas on Jesus from Borg

Looking at a variety of images of Jesus awakens one part of our brain and elicits a particular kind of response in us.

When we discuss ideas offered to us by a scholar, another part of our brain is engaged. It might be that, as we move into discussion mode, you will continue to be influenced by the images and by the part of the brain that has just been stimulated.

In this chapter, Marcus Borg tackles many significant issues about the place of Jesus at the heart of Christianity. Our intention in this course is not to "learn" all of Borg's ideas, but to be stimulated and stretched in our consideration of who Jesus is for us today.

Hand out the page "Quotes from Chapter 5."

On this handout, you will find six quotes from this chapter. They touch on some of the main ideas that Borg presents. We will use them to remind ourselves of some of the ideas in the chapter that might have caught our attention and as a springboard into discussion with one another.

Listen as they are read, watching for one or two places where your attention is particularly caught.

Begin by reading the six quotes aloud in the group, with people taking turns reading them.

When you have heard all the quotes, go around the group, allowing each person to speak to the quote(s) that had the most energy for them, saying why they think that might be the case. If you have been using the DVD for Engage 1, then play the Marcus Borg clip, "The Distinction Between 'Jesus' and 'Christ.'" This may lead into a broader discussion of the main ideas presented by Borg in this chapter.

Engage 3: Personal writing: Who Do You Say That I Am?

We have discussed ideas, we have allowed images to impact us; now, we will exercise our own creativity in response to the question of Jesus "Who do you say that I am?"

This is a writing exercise and there are two options for you to choose from: one is more "fill-in-the-blanks"; the other is more free-form and poetic.

Option 1: Sentence completion

Look at the handout "Ten Statements about Jesus that Are True for Me." You will see that the name "Jesus" is written there 10 times. Your task is to write 10 statements about Jesus that are true for you.

Option 2: Alphapoem

Look at the handout with the question, "Who do you say that I am?" written in the title at the top of the page, as well as down the side from top to bottom. The poem that you will write is your response to that question of Jesus. The limitation is that the first word of each line of the poem must begin with the letter that is already printed on the page. Start writing the first line, which must begin with a word starting with a "W." Move to the next line when you come to a word that begins with the letter "H." Keep going, dropping down a line every time you come to a word starts with the letter of the next line. Here is a model in case you need it:

When years ago you came walking into my

Home, bringing
Offerings of love, wrapped in
Dull images
Of gardens and rocks, all serious with crosses on the hillside,
You didn't tell me that I could leap
Over all those centuries of creeds and crusades
Until I
Stood with you cooking fish on
A fire beside a sea with fishing boats and
Young people ready for
The difference that they
Had tasted once
And wished would come again
To
Inspire, disturb,
Accompany, heal, bless and
Make new. Or perhaps you did and I just never heard you the way
    I do now.
?

It's hard to know how long people will need for this creative writing exercise. Probably about 15 minutes. You may have to impose a closing time at some point. You want to allow time to hear from those who are ready to read. Whether they read in small groups or in the total group depends on the size of your group and how much time you have left.

Listening to one another's writing (either the ten statements or an

alphapoem) is a sacred act. Set aside whatever you have written while you listen to the creative expressions of others.

ANTICIPATE

Think back on your life and notice times when you were "centered on God" and times when you were not. Reflect on what made the difference. Reflect also on the difference it made.

CLOSE

As we come to the end of this time of focusing on Jesus, the Heart of God, we will say again a paraphrase of the Prayer of Jesus. Let us pray together.

Alphapoem: "Who do you say that I am?"

Start writing your alphapoem on the first line, beginning with a word that starts with a "W." Drop to the next line when you come to a word that begins with the letter "H." Keep writing, dropping down a line every time you come to a word that starts with the letter of the next line.

W

H

O

D

O

Y

O

U

S

A

Y

T

H

A

T

I

A

M

?

Ten Statements about Jesus That Are True for Me

Jesus...

Jesus...

Jesus...

Jesus...

Jesus...

Jesus...

Jesus...

Jesus...

Jesus...

Jesus...

Words of Jesus

Let anyone with ears to hear listen!

Why were you searching for me?

Follow me and I will make you fish for people.

Let us go on to the neighboring towns, so that I may proclaim the message there also; for that is what I came out to do.

The Spirit of the Lord is upon me, because God has anointed me to bring good news to the poor, to proclaim release to the captives and recovery of sight to the blind, to let the oppressed go free, and to proclaim the year of the Lord's favor.

Put out into deep waters and let down your nets for a catch.

Wherever you enter a house, stay there until you leave the place.

Stretch out your hand.

Friend, your sins are forgiven you.

I say to you, stand up and take your bed and go to your home.

Blessed are you who are poor, for yours is the kingdom of God.

You give them something to eat.

You lack one thing; go, sell what you own, and give the money to the poor; then come, follow me.

What will it profit to gain the whole world and forfeit life?

Salt is good; but if salt has lost its saltiness, how can you season it? Have salt in yourselves and be at peace with one another.

Whoever wishes to become great among you must be your servant, and whoever wishes to be first among you must be slave of all.

I do choose. Be made clean!

Here are my mother and my brothers! Whoever does the will of God is my brother and sister and mother.

The realm of God is like a mustard seed, which, when sown upon the ground, is the smallest of all the seeds on earth; yet when it is sown it grows up and becomes the greatest of all shrubs…

Peace! Be still!

Who touched my clothes?

Daughter, your faith has made you well; go in peace, and be healed of your disease.

Do not fear, only believe.

Come away to a deserted place all by yourselves and rest a while.

How many loaves have you? Go and see.

Take heart, it is I; do not be afraid.

Be opened.

Why are you talking about having no bread? Are your hearts hardened? Do you have eyes, and fail to see? Do you have ears, and fail to hear?

Who do people say that I am?

Whoever welcomes one such child in my name welcomes me, and whoever welcomes me welcomes not me but the one who sent me.

What do you want me to do for you?

Let her alone; why do you trouble her? She has performed a good service for me.

I am deeply grieved, even to death; remain here, and keep awake.

Are you asleep? Could you not keep awake one hour?

Let anyone with ears to hear listen!

Why were you searching for me?

Quotes from Chapter 5
The Heart of Christianity, Marcus J. Borg

[W]henever we emphasize the divinity of Jesus at the expense of his humanity, we lose track of the utterly remarkable human being that he was. (83)

[Jesus] is the revelation, the incarnation, of God's character and passion – of what God is like and of what God is most passionate about. He shows us the heart of God. (81)

[T]he gospels contain two voices: the voice of Jesus and the voice of the community. Both layers and voices are important. The former tell us about the pre-Easter Jesus; the latter are the witness and testimony of the community to what Jesus had become in their experience in the decades after Easter. (84)

[W]e can say that [Jesus] is the decisive revelation of God for us as Christians without needing to say that he is the *only* and exclusive revelation of God, as the earlier paradigm affirms. (88–89)

In our time, many need to hear about the distinction between history and metaphor because there are many parts of the gospels that they can't take literally. When literalized, the story of Jesus becomes literally incredible. But it's not meant to be incredible; as good news, it is meant to be compelling. (84–5)

I don't think that Jesus literally died for our sins. I don't think he thought of his life and purpose that way; I don't think he thought of that as his divinely given vocation... But I do have faith in the cross as a trustworthy disclosure of the evil of domination systems, as the exposure of the defeat of the powers, as the revelation of the "way" or "path" of transformation, as the revelation of the depth of God's love for us, and as the proclamation of radical grace. (96)

SESSION

6

—

BORN AGAIN: A NEW HEART

INTEND

(This is for your guidance: you can share aspects of it with the group at any time that seems right to you.)

Outcomes for this session include the following:

❑   checking in halfway through the program to hear from participants about the impact of the program;

❑   comprehending the place of rebirth in the Christian life;

❑   exploring the concept of being "born again" as it applies to our lives;

❑   reviewing the rhythm of exile and homecoming, as we know it from our own experience;

❑   imagining what it would be like to midwife our own rebirth through spiritual practice;

❑   connecting our experience of being reborn to a gospel story;

❑   seeing our commitment to the way of Jesus through words in Paul's letters;

❑   reclaiming the language of being "born again" as a potential bridge to more conservative Christians, who have had a monopoly on that language.

PREPARE

❑   Place water and drinking glasses on a side table that is easily accessible to all.

❑   Post the "Welcome" page for people to see as they arrive.

❑   Place a candle on a central table; have matches ready.

❑   Have extra copies of the paraphrase of "The Prayer of Jesus" available (page 45).

❑   Create 13 signs, which will be posted for people to read as they arrive at the session. You will find these messages on the page called "Messages of Rebirth," (page 99). Post the signs strategically so that they are all visible to people as they enter the building and make their way to the room in which you are meeting.

❑   Make a copy of the page "Messages of Rebirth" and cut the 13 statements apart. You will need one of the statements for each person in the group, so if you have more than 13, cut up another copy of the page. Place the statements face down on the table in the center of the group.

❑   Make copies for everyone of the page "The Way of Exile and Homecoming: A Personal Journal" (page 100).

❑   Write on newsprint the instructions for the time between this session and the next. (See Anticipate section.)

WELCOME

Make sure the following words of welcome are written on newsprint and displayed in a spot where everyone can read them as they arrive:

Welcome to Session 6, Born Again: A New Heart
Find someone you haven't spent much time with in the course and talk about what you have learned from the program to this point.

OPEN

Lay out, face down on the table in the center of the group, the statements from the resource page "Messages of Rebirth." If you have more than 13 people in your group, you will have to repeat some of the statements. It is important that there be enough for each person to have one.

There are times and circumstances that would have us come to Jesus only in the dark of night.

I light this candle as an assurance of God's presence with us, even in the darkest places of our walking. (Light the candle.)

There is a time for all of us to be born of the Spirit.

I pour this, the water of birth (pour the water)**: a sign of assurance that God accompanies and welcomes us in our birth and rebirth.**

Please take from the table one of the slips of paper.

There are many ways of expressing what we mean when we speak of "rebirth." On these slips of paper are 13 different ways of speaking about rebirth. We will hear these twice during the reading of this story from the gospel of John. When I pause after reading the first four verses, we will hear all these statements, and then again at the end of the passage.

Scripture: John 3:1–10

> Now there was a Pharisee named Nicodemus, a leader of the Jews. He came to Jesus by night and said to him, "Rabbi, we know that you are a teacher who has come from God; for no one can do these signs that you do apart from the presence of God." Jesus answered him, "Very truly, I tell you, no one can see the kingdom of God without being born from above." Nicodemus said to him, "How can anyone be born after having grown old? Can one enter a second time into the mother's womb and be born?"

Go around the circle having each person read the statement of rebirth on their slip of paper.

> Jesus answered, "Very truly, I tell you, no one can enter the kingdom of God without being born of water and Spirit. What is born of the flesh is flesh, and what is born of the Spirit is spirit. Do not be astonished that I said to you, 'You must be born from

above.' The wind blows where it chooses, and you hear the sound of it, but you do not know where it comes from or where it goes. So it is with everyone who is born of the Spirit." Nicodemus said to him, "How can these things be?" Jesus answered him, "Are you a teacher of Israel, and yet you do not understand these things?"

Go around the circle and hear again the statements of rebirth on the slips of paper.

CONNECT

This is the sixth session in our program. A number of times, we have each had an indication of the impact of this book and this program on us. As we reconnect with one another in this session, let's begin by checking in about the change and transformation we are each experiencing through this learning process. This check-in happens to coincide, very appropriately, with the chapter "Born Again: A New Heart." This gives us an opportunity to see our personal learning in the context of the ideas that Borg presents in this chapter. The three questions we will respond to in this check-in are

1. What has been the impact on you of the program thus far?
2. What are you appreciating about the process of our learning and being together?
3. What questions have emerged for you as a result of being exposed to Marcus Borg's teaching and to the process of this course?

ENGAGE

Engage 1: Personal and Group Reflection on the Way of Exile and Rebirth

At the heart of this chapter, Marcus Borg leads us into a reflection on the shared human experience that takes us from birth, through exile, to rebirth. A consideration of how this applies to our own lives will be the core of our group time in this session. We will begin with a time of personal reflection using a personal journal page that has been prepared and that I will now give you. After a time of written reflection, we will gather in small groups and use our journal notes as reference for a time of sharing with one another.

Hand out copies of "The Way of Exile and Homecoming" and announce the length of time that people will have to work on this.

Depending on the size of the group, either gather in the total group or move into groups of four. This will be a time for people to share together the place that exile and homecoming have had in their lives. They can refer to both parts of the journal page, but caution participants about spending so much time on "The Road into Exile" that they don't have time to speak about "The Road of Return from Exile."

Engage 2: Exile and Rebirth in the Christian Life

Borg points out that this process of personal spiritual transformation – dying to an old self and being born into a new life in the Spirit – is central to the world's religions and not unique to Christianity. We can affirm that universality even as we live the particular "way" of Christ. In the context of this study as Christians, we don't want to lose sight of this central thesis of Borg:

> In the gospels and in the rest of the New Testament, death and resurrection, dying and rising, are again and again a metaphor for personal transformation, for the psychological-spiritual process at the center of the Christian life.
>
> – *The Heart of Christianity*, page 107

Borg makes reference to a number of verses from Paul's letters. Let's hear four selections from these letters as a way of affirming the place of our own journeys of exile and rebirth within the drama of the Christian life.

So if anyone is in Christ, there is a new creation: everything old has passed away; see, everything has become new!

— 2 Corinthians 5:17

I have been crucified with Christ; and it is no longer I who live, but it is Christ who lives in me.

— Galatians 2:19b–20a

For I am convinced that neither death, nor life, nor angels, nor rulers, nor things present, nor things to come, nor powers, nor height, nor depth, nor anything else in all creation, will be able to separate us from the love of God in Christ Jesus our Lord.

— Romans 8:38–39

If I speak in the tongues of mortals and of angels, but do not have love, I am a noisy gong or a clanging cymbal. And if I have prophetic powers, and understand all mysteries and all knowledge, and if I have all faith so as to move mountains, but do not have love, I am nothing. If I give away all my possessions, and if I hand over my body so that I may boast, but do not have love, I gain nothing.

— 1 Corinthians 13:1–3

Now return to the groups you were in previously and consider these two questions:

1. **What does it mean for you to be "born again" in the context of your commitment to the Way of Jesus?**

2. **Concerning the use of the "born again" metaphor by mainline Christians, Borg sees a potential bridge to conservative and fundamentalist Christians: "If mainline** Christians can learn to speak of the importance of being born again, the possibility that these two parts of the church might

come together increases" (page 104). **In what ways and under what circumstances could you see yourself using this metaphor?**

Engage 3: Spirituality and Rebirth

The difference between our first birth and our rebirth is that we can be conscious of this second birth and we can be intentional about it. Perhaps you remember reading these words of Marcus Borg in this chapter:

> Being born again is the work of the Spirit. Whether it happens suddenly or gradually, we can't make it happen, either by strong desire and determination or by learning and believing the right beliefs. But we can be intentional about being born again. Though we can't make it happen, we can midwife the process. This is the purpose of spirituality: to help birth the new self and nourish the new life. Spirituality is midwifery.
>
> – *The Heart of Christianity*, pages 119–120

Borg goes on to define spirituality in this way:

> Becoming conscious of and intentional about a deepening relationship with God.

What are the ways in which you become conscious of and deepen your relationship with God?

In what ways have your spiritual practices been responsible for the birth of a new self?

What else might you consider beginning as a spiritual practice during this program?

ANTICIPATE

In anticipation of the next session, pay attention to the community in which you live, asking yourself the following question: What would it look like here if God were in charge and those who govern were not?

SPECIAL NOTE TO FACILITATOR

The next session depends on having four or five members of the group prepared to talk to the whole group in response to the question: What would it mean for us to take the Kingdom of God seriously? You might want to approach some individuals at the end of this session. Marcus Borg provides four specific examples on pages 143–145: health care, the environment, economic justice, and the use of imperial power. Ask these four or five people to choose issues about which they feel some passion. Their level of expertise is not as important as the depth of their concern.

CLOSE

Have members of the group read out loud once again the 13 statements, "Messages of Rebirth."

Reconnect with God

Return home, exile

See again

Stand straight

Let go of what keeps you from God

Receive the gifts of the spirit

Center your life in God

Be compassionate as God is compassionate

Die to the old ways

Recover your true self

Live from the inside out

Die to the false self

Live into a new way of being

Let's go into the days ahead, living into the power and possibility of these calls to rebirth.

Let's go with the assurance that this community of faith accompanies us, even as the God who loves us and welcomes us home accompanies us.

And so we pray together, as is our practice, the Prayer of Jesus. Let us pray.

Messages of Rebirth

In relation to chapter six, "Born Again: A New Heart," in Marcus Borg's *The Heart of Christianity.*

Reconnect with God

Return home, exile

See again

Stand straight

Let go of what keeps you from God

Receive the gifts of the spirit

Center your life in God

Be compassionate as God is compassionate

Die to the old ways

Recover your true self

Live from the inside out

Die to the false self

Live into a new way of being

The Way of Exile and Homecoming

A PERSONAL JOURNAL PAGE

Use this page for written reflection on the themes of exile and homecoming in your own life.

The Road into Exile

Exile is an inevitable feature of the human journey that leads us from birth, through the growth of self-awareness and self-concern, and into a place where we live lives that are conferred on us by our culture more than chosen by who we are truly meant to be (page 117).

1. Recall a time in your childhood when you remember yourself as a unique child, relatively unshaped by societal, parental, cultural, and religious messages.

2. Recall a time in adolescence or early adulthood when you remember yourself as self-conscious and significantly shaped by the three A's: appearance, achievement, and affluence.

3. Recall a time in adulthood when you would say that you were living "a false self" and were exiled from your true identity.

The Road of Return from Exile

The road of return is the road of recovering true self, the path to beginning to live from the inside out rather than the outside in. Being "born again" involves dying to the false self and being born into an identity centered in God.

The born-again experience happens in many ways. Marcus Borg describes four. Personally, we may know about one or all of them. Reflecting on the born-again experience in these ways can help broaden its definition. Continue to journal on the ones that have been part of your experience, in the spaces provided below.

Four Kinds of Born-Again Experience (page 118)

1. A sudden and dramatic moment in your life (a revelation, a life-changing epiphany, a sudden conversion)

2. A gradual lifetime incremental process (experiencing the self-forgetfulness that accompanies a deepening trust in God)

3. The shorter rhythms of our lives (may occur several times in periods of major change or transition)

4. The micro-rhythms of daily life (each day forgetting God – becoming burdened – remembering God – rising from confinement)

SESSION

7

THE KINGDOM OF GOD: THE HEART OF JUSTICE

INTEND

(This is for your guidance: you can share aspects of it with the group at any time that seems right to you.)

Outcomes for this session include the following:

❏ balancing the emphasis of Session 6 on personal spirituality with attention to the political meaning of living in the Kingdom of God;

❏ learning from Jesus' way of political engagement in dealing with our real issues of injustice;

❏ imagining what a "politically engaged spirituality" might be for us;

❏ naming specific examples of what it would mean to take seriously the Kingdom of God in our community and in our world;

❏ expressing gratitude as a practice of politically engaged spirituality;

❏ deepening our shared spirituality, as we name and face the injustices of our society and our world.

PREPARE

❏ Write the words for the Carolyn McDade song *Spirit of Life* (page 103) on newsprint so that all can read it while doing simple movements to accompany it.

❑ In advance of the session, ask four or five members of the group to come prepared to talk to the whole group in response to the question, "What would it mean for us to take the Kingdom of God seriously?" Marcus Borg provides four specific examples on pages 143–145: health care, the environment, economic justice, and the use of imperial power. Ask these four or five people to choose issues about which they feel some passion. Their level of expertise is not as important as the depth of their concern.

❑ Place water and drinking glasses on a side table that is easily accessible to all.

❑ Post the "Welcome" page for people to see as they arrive.

❑ Place a candle on a central table, have matches ready.

❑ Have extra copies of the paraphrase of "The Prayer of Jesus," available (page 45).

WELCOME

Make sure the following words of welcome are written on newsprint and displayed in a spot where everyone can read them as they arrive:

Welcome to Session 7, The Kingdom of God: The Heart of Justice.
This evening let us be together in a way that witnesses to the truth of our living within the Heart of Justice.

OPEN

We don't actually have to do anything to enter the Kingdom of God, to dwell in the Heart of Justice.

We are already there. We just have to allow that truth to be the truth at the heart of our lives.

This is not a gathering of people who have to find the right road to reach the Kingdom of God. This is a gathering of people who will celebrate together the reality of being in the Heart of Justice.

We light this candle. (Light the candle.)

We are people who choose to stand in the light of God's justice.

We receive water. (Indicate the water.)

We are people who choose to receive and to share the living water of God's realm.

Let us begin with a song and movement to center us and ground us here in that truth.

Many hymnbooks have the words and music of Carolyn McDade's song *Spirit of Life,* and many people will know it by heart. However, if it is completely new to you and your group, it can be said with the actions given below.

Song with actions: *Spirit of Life, Come Unto Me,* words and music by Carolyn McDade, 1981. Used by permission.

Spirit of Life, come unto me.
> *(hands and arms stretched out and upward)*

Sing in my heart all the stirrings of compassion.
> *(hands come down and cross touching chest at the heart)*

Blow in the wind, rise in the sea;
> *(left hand makes sweeping gesture to left, right hand to the right)*

move in the hand, giving life the shape of justice.
> *(hands cupped, then rise and release justice like a bird)*

Roots hold me close; wings set me free;
> *(palms down to earth as roots, then palms up, rising as wings)*

Spirit of Life, come to me, come to me.
> *(return to start: hands and arms stretched out and upward)*

CONNECT

Paired conversations

In these four reconnecting conversations, we will name some of the things that we see in our world that call out for God's justice; we will own our own part in the systems of injustice; we will name the kinds of feelings we experience in relation to injustice; and we will speak some of our own truth about these matters.

As in previous sessions, move people into new pairs for each conversation, which will last four to five minutes.

Conversation 1

As I look around my community, my world, opening my eyes as wide as I can, I see...

Conversation 2

There are times when I know I participate in systems that contribute to the misery of others...

Conversation 3

I see so much and sometimes I wish I couldn't. The feelings can be overwhelming...

You might choose to have Conversation 4 in the total group rather than in pairs. It can act as a bridge to the "Engage" section, in which "truth-telling" could be named as a practice of Jesus. As you lead people into this next conversation, whether in pairs or in the total group, you might include in your introduction of the topic that one way we lie to ourselves is in pretending not to notice what's going on.

Conversation 4

I trust myself to know the difference between truth and lies. This is something I believe to be true today...

ENGAGE

Engage 1: Watching Jesus

Being Christian is both a call and an opportunity. We have the opportunity to become active participants in a vision and a strategy that was initiated by Jesus 2000 years ago and that still has power today. What can we learn from the way Jesus sought to bring God's kingdom to earth in his time?

Marcus Borg offers some ideas:

- Jesus spoke primarily to the peasant underclass in rural areas and he avoided cities.
- He addressed directly issues of food and debt that were the primary social issues in peasant life.
- He used the phrase Kingdom of God in a very intentional challenge to the political "kingdoms" that were such a reality for people in those days.

Imagine that you are following Jesus around, observing his behavior and his strategies. What do you notice that could make a difference for us as we become more effective agents for God's Justice? Be careful not to dis-empower yourself by saying things like, "Well, how should I know – I wasn't there!" and "I'm not a biblical scholar." Let this be an exercise of the imagination based on what you *do* remember from the Bible or from other sources. You might even give yourselves permission to be imaginative by beginning your sentences in one of these ways: "I see Jesus…," "I hear Jesus…," "I notice Jesus…"

Engage 2: Taking the Kingdom of God Seriously
In this chapter, Marcus Borg provides some of his own examples of what it would mean for Christians and residents of the United States to take the Kingdom of God seriously in our time. What would it mean for us as Canadians (Australians, Americans, Scots, etc.) to take the Kingdom of God seriously? Some members of this circle of justice-makers have given some thought during the past week to what they would say in response to that question and they are going to speak about that now.

Hear these four or five presentations.

In small groups (or in the total group if it is 12 or fewer) respond to what you heard from these five people:

- **What issue really engaged you to the point that you might do something about it?**
- **What would it mean for you, as a citizen of your country in the early 21st century, to take the Kingdom of God seriously?**

Engage 3: A Politically Engaged Spirituality
Marcus Borg writes on page 146 of *The Heart of Christianity*:

Seeing the political passion of the Bible calls us to a politically engaged spirituality... A politically engaged spirituality affirms both spiritual transformation and political transformation. The message of Jesus, and the Bible as a whole, is about both. What we see in Jesus and the Bible answers our deepest personal longing, to be born again, and the world's greatest need, the Kingdom of God.

What does a "politically engaged spirituality" look like in your life? Take that question with you from this session and work with it in the days ahead. Right now, rather than talk about it, let's take a moment to practice it. In doing this, we are anticipating the focus of Session 10, The Heart of the Matter: Practice.

We live in a culture that depends on us living with a perpetual dissatisfaction with what we have and who we are. In all kinds of ways we are told, "You don't have enough; you don't know enough; you don't drive the right car; you don't have the right clothes or even the right body; and so on and so on." To act in a way that denies that cultural message is a powerfully subversive public act. To say, "Thank you. I have enough and I am enough," is both spiritually and politically transforming. Let's practice being grateful, expressing gratitude together right now, and agree to continue practicing it individually in the days ahead.

We will simply go around the circle, with each person naming something for which they feel gratitude. We will keep going around until the time we have set has run out. Let's each use the introductory words, "I give thanks for..." (It would be ideal to have as many as five rounds so that each person expresses gratitude five times.)

At the end of the process

What do you notice from doing that?

Many people use the spiritual and political practice of beginning or ending their day by naming five things for which they give thanks. They report that, more than anything else they have done, it has transformed their attitude to the world and their capacity to act for justice.

ANTICIPATE

In the time between this session and the next, practice gratitude in the way suggested here. At the beginning of the day, name five things for which you give thanks; at the end of the day, name five things from that day for which you feel gratitude. Even though you may not be a journal writer, you might try the practice of writing these things down each time.

CLOSE

We will end this session as we began, with Carolyn McDade's song and the accompanying movements.

In parting from one another, taking a spirit of justice and compassion from this community, we will say again the paraphrase of the Prayer of Jesus. Let us pray together.

SESSION

8

—

THIN PLACES:
OPENING THE HEART

INTEND

(This is for your guidance: you can share aspects of it with the group at any time that seems right to you.)

Outcomes for this session include the following:
- ❑ reflecting on the practice of gratitude as an act of heart-opening;
- ❑ acknowledging what happens when our hearts are closed;
- ❑ using clay as a medium for expressing the opening of the heart;
- ❑ experiencing the relationship between opening ourselves physically and opening our hearts;
- ❑ considering what can make worship a time of more profound connection with God.

PREPARE

- ❑ Place a large candle on a central table, have matches ready. Also place on the table one small candle (tea lights work well) for each person in the group. These candles need to be just large enough to burn for the full time of the session.
- ❑ Bring enough 2" (5 cm) cubes of potter's clay that each person can have one piece. A local potter will be a good source. There will be a residue of clay on people's hands so have enough bowls of water and towels available that each small group of four can have water

and hand towels to share. These will be used intentionally in a community process.

❑ Before the session, practice the simple stretching movement that you will lead in the "Engage" section of this session. The instructions are thorough so that you will be able to learn the movement and lead it comfortably. Do the movement enough times so that you will feel confident when it comes to lead it. If you have never done anything like this before, take the risk to do it. Whatever you end up doing for the group will be right! Don't worry whether or not the movement is what I intended it to be. The purpose is to lead participants in a movement sequence that moves them to "open" after they have been "closed" for a while.

❑ Post the "Welcome" page for people to see as they arrive.

❑ Have extra copies of the paraphrase of the Prayer of Jesus available.

❑ Place water and drinking glasses on a side table that is easily accessible to all.

❑ Make copies of these resource pages: "I know my heart is closed…" (page 117) and "When our hearts are open…" (page 118).

❑ Write on a sheet of newsprint guidelines for the activity between this session and the next. You will find this in the "Anticipate" section.

WELCOME

Make sure the following words of welcome are written on newsprint and displayed in a spot where everyone can read them as they arrive:

Welcome to Session 8, Thin Places: Opening the Heart
Find someone to sit with and talk about something "heartfelt" that has occurred in your life since you were last here.

OPEN

The heart, a metaphor of the self at its deepest level, is the human being's spiritual center, and, as such, affects sight, thought, feeling, and will. The heart as the self can either be open, that is, turned toward God; or closed, turned away from God.

As you can see, there are enough candles here for each person to light one. Come forward, one by one, and light your candle from the central candle that I light now. As you each light your candle, say this prayer aloud or in the silence of your own heart: "O God, open my heart and let my mouth sing your praise."

In his teaching, Marcus Borg uses a prayer by an 8th-century Celtic Christian, Alcuin, to begin his session "Open Hearts and Thin Places." We will pray these ancient holy words as our opening. Let us pray...

Prayer of Alcuin
Give us, O Lord, we pray,
> firm faith,
> unwavering hope,
> a passion for justice.

Pour into our hearts
> the Spirit of Wisdom and Understanding,
> the Spirit of Counsel and Spiritual Strength,
> the Spirit of Knowledge and True Compassion,
> the Spirit of Wonder in all Your Works.

Light Eternal,
> shine in our hearts;
Power Eternal,
> deliver us from evil;
Wisdom Eternal,
> scatter the darkness of our ignorance;

Might Eternal,
> have mercy on us.

Grant that we may ever seek your face
> with all our heart, soul, and strength.

And in your infinite mercy
> bring us at last to the fullness of your presence
> where we shall behold your glory
> and live your promised joys.

In the name of Jesus,
> our body and blood,
> our life and our nourishment.

Amen.

CONNECT

In small groups

During the last session, we exercised the practice of gratitude by naming things in our lives for which we give thanks. As we reconnect here in this session, let's take time to tell one another the ways in which gratitude has been on our hearts and minds in the time between then and now.

ENGAGE

Engage 1: Uncovering the Condition of a Closed Heart

When Marcus Borg refers to a heart as closed, he means a heart that is turned away from God.

He says that when our hearts are closed these are the kinds of things that can happen:

> **We do not see clearly, nor hear.**
> **We lack understanding and have a darkened mind.**
> **We are in bondage to the desiring of our own hearts.**
> **We lack gratitude.**

We are insensitive to wonder and awe.

We forget God and lose track of mystery.

We are separated from a larger reality.

We lack compassion and do not feel the suffering of others.

We are insensitive to injustice.

Borg speaks of his awareness of times when his heart is closed. He gives specific examples: I know my heart is closed when...

I stand in a supermarket checkout line and all the people look kind of ugly.

I feel grumpy or self-preoccupied.

The world looks ordinary.

The critical voice is strong in my head.

How do you know when your heart is closed? Take the handout and complete as many of the sentence stems "I know my heart is closed when..." as you have time for. Don't put your name on the papers because I will be collecting them and you may not want me to know which is yours.

Collect these pages. Hand out the clay cubes, the bowls of water, and the hand towels.

The feel of clay may be new to you, so we will take a few minutes for you to work the clay in your hands to get used to its texture and pliability.

Now begin to shape your piece of clay to reflect the condition of a closed heart. I'm not asking you to shape something that looks like a real heart, although you could do that if you wanted to. I'm asking you to think symbolically, allowing your imagination to interact with the clay. Try not to think too hard about what you will do with it; just start working it, allowing your hands and the clay to express whatever they want.

As you do this, I will be reading some writing from the pages you have just written.

Read one item from each of the "I know my heart is closed…" pages and then go back to the beginning continuing to read from the pages in turn, until people have had the time they need with the clay.

Set aside your clay shape carefully. We will return to it shortly.

Engage 2: Open Hearts and Thin Places
Now we need to change the energy of our bodies from closed to open. We will do that in a simple movement that I will show you.

Stand comfortably, feet shoulder-width apart and hands by your side.

Hands, palms down, rise slowly in front of you until your arms are horizontal (like they are being pulled up by strings attached to the backs of your hands).

Hands, palms down, move out to each side, arms are still horizontal.

Hands rise slowly until they are above your head where your fingertips may touch, if that is comfortable for you.

Hands move out and down in a big stretch until arms are once again out horizontally at each side.

Turn hands to face forward.

Begin a gathering movement as hands and arms move in front until fingertips meet.

Turn hands so they face up and make the shape of a bowl together.

Lift hands together toward the top of your head as if the cupped hands are pouring water of blessing over your head.

Allow your open hands to move down over your face and body without actually touching it. (You will just feel the heat and energy given off by your hands as they move over your face.)

Bring your hands back to the place where they started.

Rest.

Listen to a favorite quotation of Marcus Borg's. It is the voice of Thomas Merton, a 20th-century Trappist monk, who said this about his experience of God:

"Life is this simple. We are living in a world that is absolutely transparent, and God is shining through it all the time. This is not just a fable or a nice story. It is true. If we abandon ourselves to God and forget ourselves, we see it sometimes, and we see it maybe frequently. God shows Himself everywhere, in everything – in people and in things and in nature and in events. It becomes very obvious that God is everywhere and in everything and we cannot be with God. It's impossible. The only thing is that we don't see it."

As Borg asserts, occasionally we do "see it," do experience God shining through everything. "Thin places" are places where the veil lifts between the visible world of our ordinary experience, and God, the sacred, Spirit. Close your eyes and, in the silence of this room, recall some of the "thin place" experiences of your life.

Allow several minutes for this silence and then say,

When you are ready, take the clay again.
      As you continue to reflect on the "thin place" experiences of your life, re-shape the clay to reflect the condition of your opening heart. When you are finished, place the clay on the ground in the center of the group and again wash and dry your hands.

In your small group, name together "thin places" you have experienced sometime in your life. Also, use the clay to speak about the experience of moving from a heart that is closed to God to a heart that is open to God.

In the same way he wrote about times when he was aware of his heart being closed, Borg writes about his heart being open.

Hand out the page entitled, "When our hearts are open..."

When our hearts are open...
> **We see more clearly.**
> **We move from darkness into light.**
> **We are alive to wonder.**
> **We feel profound gratitude.**
> **We feel the suffering and pain of the world and respond to it.**
> **We are compassionate as God is compassionate.**

Take time now to complete the five statements on the handout.

When people have completed this, call them back to their small groups, where they will share any new awareness they have of the condition of the open heart from their own experience.

Engage 3: Worship as a Thin Place
This is one place in this program where we have an opportunity to talk about our practice of worship. As an introduction to this, I will read the second and third paragraphs on page 157 of *The Heart of Christianity.*

What are some of the ways that enable worship to be a thin place for you? What is it about that aspect of worship that can make it a "thin place" for you? I will record your responses in point form on the newsprint and bring a collated record to our next session.

ANTICIPATE
In the time between this session and the next, observe your own heart as it moves through conditions of being open and closed. Notice your own capacity to move from a closed heart to an open heart. Continue this in a spirit of gratitude.

CLOSE

If possible, sing a hymn in closing. It might be one that someone has mentioned in the worship discussion. One suggestion would be the familiar hymn *Spirit of the Living God.*

As we come to the end of this time, we will say again the paraphrase of the Prayer of Jesus. Let us pray together.

I know my heart is closed…

when _____.

when _____.

when _____.

when _____.

when _____.

when _____.

when _____.

when _____.

when _____.

when _____.

When our hearts are open...

We see more clearly.
We move from darkness into light.
We are alive to wonder.
We feel profound gratitude.
We feel the suffering and pain of the world and respond to it.
We are compassionate as God is compassionate.

When my heart is open...

I _____

I _____

I _____

I _____

I _____

SESSION

9

SIN AND SALVATION: TRANSFORMING THE HEART

INTEND
(This is for your guidance: you can share aspects of it with the group at any time that seems right to you.)

Outcomes for this session include the following:
- ❑ reclaiming "salvation" as a way of naming our own path to wholeness;
- ❑ engaging with metaphors of salvation that illuminate our own path to Jesus, a renewed source of relationship with God;
- ❑ listening to the Psalms as human expressions of the desire for transformation of the heart;
- ❑ imagining what it would mean to "go beyond the mind you have";
- ❑ experiencing the movement to wholeness as both personal and societal;
- ❑ continuing to reflect on the condition of an open and closed heart.

PREPARE
- ❑ Place water and drinking glasses on a side table that is easily accessible to all.
- ❑ Post the "Welcome" page for people to see as they arrive.
- ❑ Place a candle on a central table; have matches ready.

❏ Have extra copies of the paraphrase of "The Prayer of Jesus,"available (page 45).

❏ Make copies of the handouts "Reclaiming 'Salvation'" (page 127) and "Metaphors of Salvation" (pages 128–129).

❏ Have a DVD player and TV or data projector ready to play the Marcus Borg clip, "Reclaiming the Word Salvation," under the "for groups" menu.

WELCOME

Make sure the following words of welcome are written on newsprint and displayed in a spot where everyone can read them as they arrive:

Welcome to Session 9, Sin and Salvation: Transforming the Heart
As you wait for the session to begin, sit with someone and talk together about places and situations where you feel a "heart" concern for our world.

OPEN

In Session 3, The Bible: The Heart of the Tradition, we had an experience of praying the scriptures in which we allowed a word or a phrase to address us individually as we listened. We will begin this session in a similar way, not as thoroughly as we did then, but still taking time to hear scripture prayerfully and to be addressed by a word or two.

You may recall that, in Chapter 8, Marcus Borg led us to think of the human heart as a metaphor for the inner self as a whole, something deeper than our perception, intellect, emotion, and will. It is the spiritual center of the self. On page 150, Borg offered selections from scripture to illustrate this comprehensive meaning of the "heart."

Here are ten other verses, all from the Psalms, that address the condition of the heart. Listen as they are read, being attentive to a word or phrase that makes a particular connection with you at this time. Let's take time now to get comfortable and relaxed. If closing your eyes helps you to listen, do so now. We will have a time of silence before I read these verses. I will pause between each selection to allow you to be fully present to the words and the response they elicit in you.

Search me, O God, and know my heart… *Psalm 139:23a*

Turn to me and be gracious to me, for I am lonely and afflicted. Relieve the troubles of my heart, and bring me out of my distress. *Psalm 25:16–17*

My heart throbs, my strength fails me; as for the light of my eyes – it also has gone from me. *Psalm 38:10*

Teach me your way, O God, that I may walk in your truth; give me an undivided heart to revere your name. *Psalm 86:11*

Create in me a clean heart, O God, and put a new and right spirit within me. *Psalm 51:10*

Those who…speak the truth from their heart…shall never be moved. *Psalm 15:2b, 5b*

I will give thanks to God with my whole heart. *Psalm 9:1*

I will walk with integrity of heart within my house… *Psalm 101:2b*

Trust in God at all times, O people; pour out your heart before God. God is a refuge for us. *Psalm 62:8*

Let the words of my mouth and the meditation of my heart be acceptable to you, O God, my rock and my redeemer. *Psalm 19:14*

Amen.

A word or a line from those verses may have stood out for you. Hold on to those words, focusing on them as I light the candle. (Light the candle.)

This light burns persistently at the heart of our community of learning and growing together.

This light reminds us, as we speak together, that we are held by the buoyancy of God.

This light joins our own hearts that open now to continue the adventure of faith and passion.

There is light for you and there is water. Be refreshed and be blessed!

CONNECT

We will continue our practice of reconnecting in small group conversation. There are two things you might choose to share together.

1. Share a personal reflection emerging from listening to the verses from the Psalms we just heard, including, if you choose, sharing the word, or words, which spoke to you.
2. Thinking back to last week's session "Thin Places: Opening the Heart," talk about a time since the last session when you have experienced the difference between having a closed heart and an open heart. Can you recall and describe a time when you actually felt the shift from your heart being closed to it being open? What is that like for you when it happens?

If you collated responses to last week's conversation "Worship as a Thin Place," this would be an appropriate time to hand those out and to allow for observations.

ENGAGE

Engage 1: Sin and Salvation Overview

The handout "Reclaiming 'Salvation'" presents ten key assertions that Marcus Borg makes in this chapter. They provide an opportunity for a *quick review* of the main points in a chapter that might have been the most challenging so far in terms of theological concepts and ideas. If you have access to a DVD player and TV or data projector, then play the Marcus Borg clip, "Reclaiming the Word Salvation for Emerging

Times," in which he addresses this topic. A short discussion of the issues raised by Marcus Borg in the book and on the DVD will follow, however, *be careful not to get bogged down in an intellectual discussion of sin and salvation.* The process to follow is *the most important part of this session* and will provide an experiential way of living into the question of salvation as it applies to our lives today.

Engage 2: Living Metaphors of Salvation

A number of times in this chapter, Marcus Borg makes reference to the exodus of the people of Israel from the land of Egypt. He offers it as an example of one of the "macro-stories" of scripture, which depict a human problem in story form. We don't have time to hear the whole story of the exodus, but we can look in on one brief episode in that journey, which took them out of slavery and into a wilderness. The people of Israel are free of the Egyptians. Now they have to deal with the realities of a new and unfamiliar freedom. Little do they know that it will take them 40 years to shake loose their identity as slaves.

Listen to this episode in the journey from Exodus 17:1–7.

From the wilderness of Sin the whole congregation of the Israelites
    journeyed by stages,
as GOD commanded.
They camped at Rephidim,
but there was no water for the people to drink.
The people quarreled with Moses, and said, "Give us water to
    drink."
Moses said to them, "Why do you quarrel with me? Why do you test
    our GOD?"
But the people thirsted there for water;
and the people complained against Moses and said,
"Why did you bring us out of Egypt, to kill us and our children and
    livestock with thirst?"

So Moses cried out to GOD,

"What shall I do with this people? They are almost ready to stone me."

GOD said to Moses,

"Go on ahead of the people, and take some of the elders of Israel with
  you;

take in your hand the staff with which you struck the Nile, and go.

I will be standing there in front of you on the rock at Horeb.

Strike the rock, and water will come out of it, so that the people may
  drink."

Moses did so, in the sight of the elders of Israel.

He called the place Massah and Meribah,

because the Israelites quarreled and tested GOD, saying, "Is GOD
  among us or not?"

The conditions described in that Bible story were very real for those people. They really were thirsty and their need for water was satisfied. Moses really *was* helpless and his need for a solution was satisfied. In this chapter, Marcus Borg helps us to see the reality of our human dilemmas in a way that doesn't require us to see ourselves as sinners needing forgiveness. That might be one human condition: we might have done wrong and we might need to ask forgiveness of someone. But there are numerous other conditions like thirst and captivity that are real and not entirely of our own making. Salvation is a process by which we can move from a condition that is a problem to a place of health and wholeness. For the thirsty, there can be water. For the helpless, there can be support.

The second handout "Metaphors of Salvation" provides a framework for personal exploration of the path to wholeness.

The steps in this process of personal exploration are outlined in the worksheet that I will give you now.

Hand out copies of the "Metaphors of Salvation: Worksheet."

You will notice that the process is repeated, once with a personal emphasis, and the second time with a social one. You will recall from your reading in this chapter that Marcus Borg is very clear that the journey to wholeness is both social and personal.

When people have had enough time to complete the worksheet, call them together in pairs or in groups of four to share where their written reflection led them.

When they have had enough time in the small groups or in pairs (at least five minutes per person), call them back to the total group and invite people to share insights from the process they have just completed.

Engage 3: Going Beyond the Mind You Have

Remind the group of the ways that Marcus Borg talks about repentance.

Repentance is…

- returning from exile and reconnecting with God,
- going beyond the mind you have, the one you have been given or acquired,
- the path of transformation, of being born again,
- following the Way of Jesus.

Based on the conversation you just had in the small groups and these ways of thinking about repentance, what would it look like for you "to go beyond the mind you have" at this time in your faith journey?

ANTICIPATE

Between this session and the next, notice what you do in the everyday that helps you to pay attention to God.

CLOSE

As we come to the end of this time of learning in community, we will say again, as is our practice, the paraphrase of the Prayer of Jesus. Let us pray together.

Reclaiming "Salvation"
Transformation as a Way of Life

TEN KEY BORG ASSERTIONS CONCERNING SALVATION

1. Using the word "sin" as a blanket term for all that ails us as humans, some of which need forgiveness, is not as helpful as naming specific predicaments of the human condition that need transformation.

2. Our understanding of the Christian vision of life is enriched by using multiple biblical images for the human problem and its remedy.

3. Salvation in its broadest sense means becoming whole and being healed.

4. The Bible is not about the saving of individuals for heaven, but about a new social and personal reality in the midst of this life.

5. Jesus' message was about a way of transformation in this world and the Kingdom of God on earth, not about how to get to heaven.

6. The "macro-stories" of scripture, such as the Exodus from Egypt and the Exile in Babylon, present the biblical meanings of salvation.

7. The New Testament understandings of Jesus correlate with the macro-stories of the Hebrew Bible. The story of Jesus thus becomes a story of salvation.

8. Salvation is not only personal; it is also social. It is about the wholeness of a community living together in peace and justice.

9. Salvation is the work of God, but without our response, little or nothing will change in our lives or in the life of the world.

10. Repentance is the resolve to go beyond the "mind" that has been shaped by culture, to a "mind" that is Christ-centered. It is the path of salvation.

METAPHORS OF SALVATION

Predicaments in the Human Condition	What We Need for Wholeness	Jesus as our Source of New Relationship with God
captivity	liberation	our liberator
exile	to return home	Jesus is our way of return
being lost	a way	our door, our way
blindness	to see	light of the world
hunger	satisfaction for hunger	bread of life
thirst	quenching of thirst	living water
having a closed heart	to open our hearts	a heart of compassion
separation from God	to connect to the source of life	our way to God, the vine
living a false self	to die and to be born again	our path of dying and rising
infirmity	healing	the one who makes us whole

Metaphors of Salvation:
Worksheet

A. PERSONAL

1. Look down the left-hand column, "Predicaments in the Human Condition." Is there one of those dilemmas that is real *for you now, or has been real at some point in your life?* Make a note of it here, describing in a sentence or two the nature of that predicament.

2. Look at the middle column, "What We Need for Wholeness." Write in the space below what that need feels like; what it's like to live with the absence of something to fill this need.

3. Go to the third column, "Jesus as Our Source of New Relationship with God." Write a short prayer that expresses the desire inherent in the statement you have chosen. Begin the prayer by naming the hope you see offered by God through Jesus. For example: "O God, light of the world…" or "Holy One, you who loves us as we are and who makes us whole…"

B. SOCIETAL

1. Look down the left-hand column, "Predicaments in the Human Condition." Is there one of those dilemmas that is real for *our society or world* right now? Make a note of it here, describing in a sentence or two the nature of that predicament.

2. Look at the middle column, "What We Need for Wholeness." Write in the space below what that need feels like; what it's like for you to live in a society or world with the absence of something to fill this need.

3. Go to the third column, "Jesus as Our Source of New Relationship with God." Write a short prayer for your society, your world, which expresses the desire inherent in the statement you have chosen. Begin the prayer by naming the hope you see offered by God through Jesus. For example: "O God, light of the world…" or "Holy One, you who loves us as we are and who makes us whole…"

SESSION

10

THE HEART OF THE MATTER: PRACTICE

INTEND

(This is for your guidance: you can share aspects of it with the group at any time that seems right to you.)

Outcomes for this session include the following:
- ❑ inviting members of the group to pay more attention to God, through the deepening of their practice of the Christian Way;
- ❑ paying attention to God through scripture using an ages-old discipline of centering and prayer;
- ❑ exploring what "practice" means for us personally and communally;
- ❑ asking how we might live a practice of compassion and justice;
- ❑ using the metaphor of a quilt to visualize a communal approach to making a difference in the world;
- ❑ deepening our sense of practice as a way of shaping our Christian identity;
- ❑ experiencing nurture through practice.

PREPARE

- ❑ Make copies of the scripture passages that are to be read during the time of opening so that people in the group can participate in reading them aloud. You will find them on the pages called "Scripture on Practice," (page 139–140).

❏ Make copies of "Practicing Practice" (page 141), a page participants will need to refer to on two occasions during the session.

❏ Bring newsprint and markers for recording the practices named by the group.

❏ Bring a large piece of plain cotton fabric to cover a tabletop. Cut out 4" to 6" (10 to 15 cm) squares of variously colored paper on which people will write. Have some colored markers available for writing on the squares of paper. The participants will place the squares of fabric on the material to resemble a quilt. Have straight pins on hand so that at the end of the exercise the paper can be pinned on the fabric and hung on the wall.

❏ Place water and drinking glasses on a side table that is easily accessible to all.

❏ Post the "Welcome" page for people to see as they arrive.

❏ Place a candle on a central table; have matches ready.

❏ Have extra copies of the paraphrase of "The Prayer of Jesus," available (page 45).

❏ Have a DVD player and TV or data projector ready to play the Marcus Borg clip, "Practices for Living the Transition," under the "for groups" menu. You will be using it in Engage 1.

WELCOME

Make sure the following words of welcome are written on newsprint and displayed in a spot where everyone can read them as they arrive:

Welcome to Session 10, The Heart of the Matter: Practice
As you wait for the session to begin, sit in silence, practicing attentiveness to yourself and to others as they arrive and prepare for this session.

OPEN

Before you begin, hand out the pages "Scripture On Practice." Participants will need this handout during the opening time.

As we begin this tenth session, which focuses on practice, we will continue our practice of lighting the candle that is here in the midst of our community.

I light this candle, one more sacred flame in the heavenly glow of candle flames that have illuminated your holy path. (Light the candle.)

I pour this water and invite you to continue our practice of taking water as you need it and of offering refreshment to others as a sign of our hospitality and care for one another. (Pour the water.)

Practice is about the formation of our Christian identity. The Bible plays a special role in this. Its stories, visions, and dreams shape our sense of who God is, who we are, and what life is about.

As we begin this session on practice, let's hear some verses from scripture that emphasize the significance of practice in enabling us to pay attention to God more fully. You will find these verses on the handout, "Scripture on Practice." We will go around the circle, sharing in the reading. If you don't want to read just say, "Pass."

CONNECT

Paired conversations

(These instructions are included on the page "Practicing Practice," which you can hand out now.)

Conversation 1

Borg quote: *Practice is paying attention to God. (page 189)*
Question for conversation: What practices enable you to pay attention to God more fully? What happens as a result of your paying attention to God?

Conversation 2

Borg quote: *Practice is about the formation of who we are as Christians, our Christian identity... (page 190)*

Question for conversation: What practices enable you to sustain a Christian identity as distinct from an identity given by the "world"?

Conversation 3

Borg quote: *Practice is not simply something we do. Rather, it nourishes us. (page 192)*

Question for conversation: What practices nourish you? What does it actually feel like to be "nourished" through practice?

ENGAGE

Engage 1: What Is "Practice" for Us?

Marcus Borg goes into some detail in this chapter on what is included in his Christian practice. You've just been talking about aspects of your practice in the paired conversations. Let's gather in the total group and make a group list of all the things that this community of Christian practitioners would include in its understanding of practice. I'll record these on newsprint as you name them.

When there are no more contributions, continue...

As you look over this list of practices...
- **Are there some that are new to you as practices?**
- **Are you thinking about "practice" in any new ways?**
- **Are there some that you feel attracted to making a part of your life practices? How would you go about that?**

If you have access to a DVD player and TV or data projector, then play the Marcus Borg clip, "Practices for Living the Transition," in which he presents some practices for living faithfully in this time of transition in the Christian community. Before going on to Engage 2, allow time for people to express their responses to Borg's suggestions. Which practices have the potential of supporting you in this time of change and transtion?

Engage 2: Centering Practice and Praying Scripture

This is a guided meditation. Take your time reading it. It's far better to err on the side of "slow" than to risk rushing.

Get comfortable where you are sitting.

If it is comfortable for you to close your eyes during a meditation, then do so now.

Become relaxed by breathing deeply three times.

Check your body for places of tension and breathe relaxation into those places.

The road you have traveled this day has included places that were gentle and creative as well as places that were rough and bumpy.

If you are holding a memory of bumpiness somewhere in your body, let it go.

Welcome the memory of the gentle and creative places of this day.

Go to the memory of those places that have fed you, body and soul.

In your heart, express your gratitude to God for them.

Was there a time today when you were particularly aware of God accompanying you?

Was there a time today when you were particularly aware of being attentive to God?

A poet from the Hebrew scriptures wrote one of the most resonant and repeated poems of all time from an awareness of God's nurturing and compassionate presence in life.

Hear again the words of Psalm 23, which present us with a metaphor of God as a shepherd and a host. As you listen, be attentive for a word or a line that stands out for you.

Read Psalm 23. The version below is an inclusive translation from the Hebrew, published in *Songs for the Holy One: Psalms and Refrains for Worship,* by Thomas Barnett and Donald Patriquin.

Holy One, you are my shepherd,
    therfore I can lack nothing.
You make me lie down in green pastures;
    you lead me beside restful waters.
You restore my soul;
    you guide along the right path, for your name's sake.
Even though I go through a valley of deadly darkness,
    I fear no evil, for you are with me;
    your crook and staff comfort and support me.
You spread a table for me in the presence of my foes.
You annoint my head with oil; my cup is overflowing.
Truly goodness, love, and loyalty follow me all my life long.
Holy One, I shall dwell in your house for days without end.
                     – (*Songs for the Holy One,* Wood Lake Books, 2004)

Hear inside yourself the word or line that stood out from the psalm.

    Repeat it slowly allowing it to interact with your inner world of concerns, memories, and feelings.

    Allow this word or phrase to be God's word for you in this moment.

    Linger with it, repeating it, and letting it touch you at the deepest level.

    There will be a time of silence while you do that.

Silence

Speak to God. Whether you use words, ideas, images, or all three is not important.

Meet with God as you would with one who loves and accepts you.

Offer to God what you have discovered in yourself during the reflection on the word or phrase from the psalm.

Experience God using the word or phrase that has been given as a means of blessing you.

Allow your real self to be touched and changed by the word of God.

There will be another time of silence.

Silence

Rest in God's embrace.

Feel gratitude in the knowledge that God is with you in both words and silence.

Experience restfulness in the presence of the One who loves you.

Thank God for whatever you have received in this time of holy conversation.

Once again, breathe deeply three times.

Return gently from this time of meditation. There is no need to hurry.

As you feel ready, come back to the light of this room, to the presence of others around you.

This will be a powerful experience for many people. Leave time for people to talk about any aspect of the practice that they would like to. Monitor your time so that you leave enough time to experience the next section on the practice of justice and compassion.

Engage 3: Practicing Compassion and Justice

Borg proposes, very precisely, ways of engaging in a practice of compassion and justice. Here are some of his suggestions:

- ❑ have direct contact with the poor and disadvantaged,
- ❑ be thoughtful about the positions of political leaders and be an informed participant in the public arena,
- ❑ increase giving until 50 percent goes to organizations whose purpose is to make change in the name of justice,
- ❑ initiate a group in your congregation to study and make recommendations to the congregation on humanitarian organizations, whose purpose is transformation and not simply aid.

Borg introduces us to a metaphor offered by Sallie McFague, a contemporary theologian, who compared our task of practicing compassion and justice to women gathering to make a patchwork quilt. "Nobody is responsible for doing the whole quilt; rather, it is the product of a host of people working together. The important thing is for each of us to do our patch."

Let's try creating our own patchwork quilt. Here are some squares of paper. On each square, write either one activity of compassion and justice-making that you already practice, or one that you would commit to take on. You can write on as many squares as you choose.

When people have had enough time, gather around the table where the cotton fabric has been spread out.

Now we will "practice" our imaginary needlework skills by creating our quilt! As we stand around the table and the fabric, we will take turns placing our squares, reading what we have written as we do so. You can offer your squares all at once or you can do one at a time, as you feel moved. Be aware of the growth of our community justice quilt as it grows from nothing. Notice your contributions filling in spaces in the quilt of community.

ANTICIPATE

As you live through the time between this session and the next, think about your response to the question, "Why are you a Christian?"

CLOSE

In our closing this evening, we will read (sing) together the words of the prophet Micah.

If you know the music and words that Jim Strathdee wrote based on this passage, then use them. It's another very inspiring way to experience community as a place of support for justice makers.

> What does the Lord require of you,
> but to do justice,
> and to love kindness,
> and to walk humbly with your God
>
> – Micah 6:8

As we come to the end of our exploration of the power of practice in our lives, we will give ourselves once more to our practice of praying the Prayer of Jesus. Let us pray together.

Scripture on Practice

Practice is about the formation of our Christian identity. The Bible plays a special role in this. Its stories, visions, and dreams shape our sense of who God is, who we are, and what life is about. As we begin this session on practice, let's hear some verses from scripture that emphasize the significance of practice in enabling us to pay attention to God more fully.

As God's chosen ones, holy and beloved, clothe yourselves with compassion, kindness, humility, meekness, and patience. Bear with one another and, if anyone has a complaint against another, forgive each other; just as the Lord has forgiven you, so you also must forgive. Above all, clothe yourselves with love, which binds everything together in perfect harmony. *Colossians 3:12–14*

When an alien resides with you in your land, you shall not oppress the alien. The alien who resides with you shall be to you as the citizen among you; you shall love the alien as yourself, for you were aliens in the land of Egypt: I am the LORD your God. *Leviticus 19:33–34*

Then turning toward the woman, he said to Simon, "Do you see this woman? I entered your house; you gave me no water for my feet, but she has bathed my feet with her tears and dried them with her hair. You gave me no kiss, but from the time I came in she has not stopped kissing my feet. You did not anoint my head with oil, but she has anointed my feet with ointment. Therefore, I tell you, her sins, which were many, have been forgiven; hence she has shown great love. But the one to whom little is forgiven, loves little." *Luke 7:44–47*

Do not be conformed to this world, but be transformed by the renewing of your minds, so that you may discern what is the will of God – what is good and acceptable and perfect. *Romans 12:2*

Then Peter came and said to him, "Lord, if another member of the church sins against me, how often should I forgive? As many as seven times?" Jesus said to him, "Not seven times, but, I tell you, seventy-seven times." *Matthew 18:21–22*

I call heaven and earth to witness against you today that I have set before you life and death, blessings and curses. Choose life so that you and your descendants may live. *Deuteronomy 30:19*

Remember the Sabbath day, and keep it holy. Six days you shall labor and do all your work. But the seventh day is a Sabbath to the LORD your God; you shall not do any work – you, your son or your daughter, your male or female slave, your livestock, or the alien resident in your towns. For in six days the LORD made heaven and earth, the sea, and all that is in them, but rested the seventh day; therefore the LORD blessed the Sabbath day and consecrated it. *Exodus 20:8–11*

Then I said, "Ah, GOD! Truly I do not know how to speak, for I am only a boy." But God said to me, "Do not say, 'I am only a boy'; for you shall go to all to whom I send you, and you shall speak whatever I command you. Do not be afraid of them, for I am with you to deliver you, says the God." Then God put out his hand and touched my mouth; and God said to me, "Now I have put my words in your mouth." *Jeremiah 1:6–9*

So then, putting away falsehood, let all of us speak the truth to our neighbors, for we are members of one another. Be angry but do not sin; do not let the sun go down on your anger, and do not make room for the devil. Thieves must give up stealing; rather let them labor and work honestly with their own hands, so as to have something to share with the needy. Let no evil talk come out of your mouths, but only what is useful for building up, as there is need, so that your words may give grace to those who hear. *Ephesians 4:25–29*

Are any among you sick? They should call for the elders of the church and have them pray over them, anointing them with oil in the name of the Lord. The prayer of faith will save the sick, and the Lord will raise them up; and anyone who has committed sins will be forgiven. *James 5:14–15*

Let the word of Christ dwell in you richly; teach and admonish one another in all wisdom; and with gratitude in your hearts sing psalms, hymns, and spiritual songs to God. *Colossians 3:16*

Practicing Practice

During this session there will be times when you will need to make reference to the material printed on this page.

PAIRED CONVERSATIONS

Conversation 1
Borg quote: *Practice is paying attention to God. (page 189)*
Question for conversation: What practices enable you to pay attention to God more fully? What happens as a result of your paying attention to God?

Conversation 2
Borg quote: *Practice is about the formation of who we are as Christians, our Christian identity. (page 190)*
Question for conversation: What practices enable you to sustain a Christian identity as distinct from an identity given by the "world"?

Conversation 3
Borg quote: *Practice is not simply something we do. Rather, it nourishes us. (page192)*
Question for conversation: What practices nourish you? What does it actually feel like to be "nourished" through practice?

CLOSING

What does the Lord require of you,
but to do justice,
and to love kindness,
and to walk humbly with your God
— Micah 6:8

11

HEART AND HOME: BEING CHRISTIAN IN AN AGE OF PLURALISM

INTEND

(This is for your guidance: you can share aspects of it with the group at any time that seems right to you.)

Outcomes for this session include the following:

❑ being challenged to name why we are Christian;
❑ looking at the implications of living as Christians in an age of pluralism;
❑ gaining a sacramental understanding of religion;
❑ allowing sacred writing to remind us of who we are and where we come from;
❑ recognizing how the landscape of pluralism is changing rapidly;
❑ being in community to support one another in times of dramatic change.

PREPARE

❑ Place water and drinking glasses on a side table that is easily accessible to all.
❑ Post the "Welcome" page for people to see as they arrive.
❑ Place a candle on a central table; have matches ready.

❑ Have extra copies of the paraphrase of the Prayer of Jesus available.

❑ Make copies of the handout "Jerusalem! Psalm 122" (page 149) and "Heart and Home" (page 150).

❑ Make copies of the "Program Evaluation Form" (pages 151–152) and have them ready to hand out at the end of this session so that people can respond to it prior to the next session.

❑ Have a DVD player and TV or data projector ready to play the Marcus Borg clip, "Emerging Christianity in a Pluralistic World," under the "for groups" menu. You will be using it in Engage 1.

WELCOME

Make sure the following words of welcome are written on newsprint and displayed in a spot where everyone can read them as they arrive:

Welcome to Session 11, Heart and Home: Being Christian in an Age of Pluralism
While you are waiting for the session to begin, talk with someone in the group about ways in which you have both continued to practice "paying attention to God."

OPEN

For this opening time, people will need a copy of the handout "Jerusalem! Psalm 122." Before beginning to read this opening, identify which is the "right" side of the group and which is the "left" side.

People have for thousands of years
    sought out and built sacred places,
    sanctuaries and shrines.
In these places, their spirits have been renewed.
They have reached across the boundary of the visible and invisible
    to touch the holy mystery of life.

They have been inspired to live in community with compassion.
They have released the burdens of their living
    and welcomed holy healing light.
They have danced and sung their stories.
They have lit fires, torches, and candles. (Light the candle.)
They have poured out living water in gratitude. (Pour the water.)
They have raised their voices in prayer and praise together.

Read the handout "Jerusalem! Psalm 122" together.

When we read this psalm together, we are reading literature of a religious community that existed long before the Christian era. Our Jewish friends continue to live this ancient tradition, of which the Psalms are a part. Hebrew scriptures are part of our tradition, too.

Pilgrims who have followed the path of faith from Abraham and Sarah have shaped three different sacred stories: Judaism, Islam, and Christianity. Those pilgrims still ascend to the Holy City where they pray, according to their own practice and tradition, for Jerusalem's peace and well-being.

In this session, we gather as a community of Christians who are called to recognize the pluralism of this 21st-century world in which we live, called to embrace in more profound ways the faith perspective of others, called to claim the spiritual and religious "home" which is ours.

Let us set out on this journey with open hearts and holy curiosity…

CONNECT

Marcus Borg quotes statistics from a poll taken in the United States in 2002. As we begin our exploration of religious pluralism, let's use the same polling questions within this group. Just raise your hand in response to each of these categories:

1. Those of you who personally know somebody who is Christian.
2. Those of you who personally know somebody who is Jewish.
3. Those of you who personally know somebody who is Muslim.
4. Those of you who personally know somebody who is Hindu.
5. Those of you who personally know somebody who is Buddhist.
6. Those of you who personally know somebody who is Sikh.

Talk with one other person about the results of this group poll. If you had been involved in the same poll in 1990, how different would your response have been?

ENGAGE

Engage 1: Emerging Christianity in a Pluralistic World

If you have access to a DVD player and TV or data projector, then play the Marcus Borg clip, "Emerging Christianity in a Pluralistic World." Take time to respond to what you hear either in pairs, groups of four, or in the total group.

Engage 2: The Sacramental Understanding of Religion

Because we are faced with the growing reality of religious pluralism, it is important that we think through some of the implications and opportunities of that new reality. Beginning on page 213, Marcus Borg offers us seven statements that describe the sacramental understanding of religion, an understanding that is consistent with the vision of emerging Christianity, which is at the heart of this book.

Listen to the seven statements as I read them twice. Note your response to each, but particularly to the overall understanding of religion generated by all seven together.

The sacramental understanding of religion sees religions as

1. human creations or "imaginative human constructions,"

2. responses to experiences of the sacred in the cultures into which they came into being,

3. cultural-linguistic traditions within which the faithful live,

4. wisdom traditions deeply rooted in the past, which enshrine wisdom of "the real" and "the way,"

5. aesthetic traditions that value and create beauty,

6. communities of practice that provide practical means for living the religious life,

7. communities of transformation: transforming self to a new way, and the world through compassion.

In summary, Marcus Borg writes the following:

The enduring religions share these characteristics in common. Each is a massive and magnificent sacrament of the sacred, a finite means of mediating the sacred, a "treasure in earthen vessels." Each of the enduring religions is a mediator of "the absolute," but not "absolute" itself. (page 215)

Have small groups of three or four discuss the following questions: What is your "heart" response to hearing this way of seeing all the enduring religions of the world? What does this understanding of religion offer you? Is there anything you would do differently as a result of hearing these seven characteristics?

Engage 3: Heart and Home
Hand out the page entitled "Heart and Home."

Marcus Borg writes with passion about why he is a Christian. This handout presents words from the last three pages of Chapter 11.

Read aloud the handout "Heart and Home."

Following Borg's lead, we are going to take time to write our own statements of heart and home. Your subtitle might be the same as Borg's: "Why I'm a Christian." Or it might be another subtitle, one that represents what is true for you, such as, "Why I am not a Christian," or "Why I want to become a Christian."

After people have had enough time to write their statements, move into either the total group or small groups.

This is a time to hear the statements you have just written, from those who are ready to offer them. The last session focused on practice. What we are doing now is engaging in the practice of witnessing one another, as we make declarations of belief and faith. Let's listen to one another with attentive hearts, setting aside judgment, and receiving these heartfelt statements in a spirit of loving accompaniment.

Engage 4: Implications
In small groups:

We have considered many matters in this session. Our final task is to respond to this question: What are the implications of being Christian in an age of pluralism? Have someone in your group record the points you come up with. We'll hear some of them in the total group and we'll collate all the contributions into a handout that you will receive in our final session.

Bring responses to total group: gather them on newsprint, allowing for response and discussion in the larger group.

ANTICIPATE

The next session will be the final one. Rather than take time during the next session to fill out the evaluation form for the course, I am giving them to you this week and asking that you take time to complete them and bring them to the next session.

CLOSE

In closing, we return to the psalm with which we began the session. It contains within it so much of what has been our concern in this session:

- ❑ **the desire and intention to praise God,**
- ❑ **the peace greeting, which we offer beyond our family and friends,**
- ❑ **the holy place, steeped in sacred story, where pilgrims will be drawn for all time,**
- ❑ **the call from the community to go to the sanctuary of the Holy One,**
- ❑ **the interweaving of faith stories, whose pilgrims find themselves praying on the same stones,**
- ❑ **the reality of desire and change: irresistible, inevitable, often painful, always blessed.**

Read together again "Jerusalem! Psalm 122."

As we come to the end of this time, we will say again, as is our practice, the prayer that speaks of our home in Christ, the Prayer of Jesus. Let us pray together.

Jerusalem!
Psalm 122

Left: I was delighted when people said to me,
"Let's go to the temple of the Holy One!"

Right: Now our feet are standing
in your gates, O Jerusalem.

All: **We pray for peace in Jerusalem and in our world.**

Left: Jerusalem! Built as a perfect city
where pilgrims gather in unity.

Right: Whither the tribes ascend,
tribes of the Holy One,
as ordained for Israel,

Left: "Give thanks to the Holy One's Name!"

Right: Thrones of judgment are there,
thrones of David's heirs.

Left: Pray for Jerusalem's peace and well-being:

Right: "May there be peace within your walls
and prosperity in your palaces."

Left: For the sake of my family and friends
I say, "Peace be with you!"

Right: For the sake of the temple of our mighty God,
I pray for your well-being.

All: **We pray for peace in Jerusalem and in our world.**

– From *Songs for the Holy One: Psalms and Refrains for Worship,*
by Thomas Barnett and Donald Patriquin
(Wood Lake Books, 2004). Used by permission.

Heart and Home: "Why I'm a Christian"
Marcus J. Borg

The Christian tradition is familiar; it is "home" for me.
I was born into it and grew up in it.
Its stories, language, music, and ethos are familiar.
It nurtured me.

I have grown to appreciate its extraordinary richness:
its antiquity and wisdom;
the beauty of its language and music and forms of worship;
its passion for compassion and justice;
the sheer goodness of its most remarkable lives.

Its worship nourishes me;
its hymns move me;
its scripture and theology engage my imagination and thought;
its practices shape me.

For me, it mediates the good, the true, and the beautiful;
and through all these, it mediates the sacred.
It is, for me, a sacrament of the sacred.

And it is home.
It is familiar to me in a way that no other religion could ever become.
Had I been born a Buddhist or a Muslim or a Jew…I am quite sure I would still be one.
But for me, Christianity is "home" like no other tradition could be.
For me, the ethos of Christianity –
    its vision and way of life,
    its scripture, worship, language, music, thought, vision, and so forth – is home.

Home is about more than familiarity and comfort.
Home is also about growing up,
    about maturation,
    about learning and living a way of life that one takes into the larger world.
Christianity is a way of life; that is its heart.
To be Christian means living "the path" within this tradition.

At the heart of Christianity is the way of the heart –
    a path that transforms us at the deepest level of our being.
At the heart of Christianity is the heart of God –
    a passion for our transformation and the transformation of the world.
At the heart of Christianity is participating in the passion of God.

– From *The Heart of Christianity: Rediscovering a Life of Faith* (San Francisco: HarperSanFrancisco, 2003), pp. 223–225.

Evaluation
Experiencing the Heart of Christianity
A 12-Session Program for Groups

1. Elements of the Program
What kind of difference did these things make for you in your learning and growing in the program?

	Small difference			**Moderate**			**Huge Difference**		

Small group discussion 1   2   3   4   5   6   7   8   9   10

Comment:

Using a published text 1   2   3   4   5   6   7   8   9   10

Comment:

Meeting for 12 sessions 1   2   3   4   5   6   7   8   9   10

Comment:

Experiential learning 1   2   3   4   5   6   7   8   9   10

Comment:

The meeting space 1   2   3   4   5   6   7   8   9   10

Comment:

Variety in sessions 1   2   3   4   5   6   7   8   9   10

Comment:

(other)_____ 1   2   3   4   5   6   7   8   9   10

Comment:

2. Specific Topics by Chapter

Place a number, from **1** (not much connection) to **5** (very powerful connection), beside each chapter topic in relation to its connection with you at this stage of your faith journey.

1. The Heart of Christianity in a Time of Change   _____
2. Faith: The Way of the Heart   _____
3. The Bible: The Heart of the Tradition   _____
4. God: The Heart of Reality   _____
5. Jesus: The Heart of God   _____
6. Born Again: A New Heart   _____
7. The Kingdom of God: The Heart of Justice   _____
8. Thin Places: Opening the Heart   _____
9. Sin and Salvation: Transforming the Heart   _____
10. The Heart of the Matter: Practice   _____
11. Heart and Home: Being Christian in an Age of Pluralism   _____

3. Feedback to Facilitator (Please comment on the effectiveness of the following)

Group Facilitation:

Program Emphasis for each week:

Variety of Activities offered:

Use of the space:

Worship:

Other: _____

4. The Difference it made for you (a testimonial)

Borg's subtitle is *Rediscovering a Life of Faith…How We Can Be Passionate Believers Today*
What difference has taking this course made in your life of faith?

Can we use this statement with your name when we promote the program? **Yes ___ No ___**

Your Name _____
(Please feel free to attach an additional page of comments.)

SESSION

12

IN THE END: A NEW BEGINNING

INTEND

(This is for your guidance: you can share aspects of it with the group at any time that seems right to you.)

Outcomes for this session include the following:
- ❑ bringing closure to this program;
- ❑ evaluating several aspects of the program;
- ❑ celebrating and closing the community of learners;
- ❑ expressing appreciation to Marcus Borg for the gifts that he gave through his book;
- ❑ reflecting on the difference this program has made in our learning and growth;
- ❑ appreciating the learning community of which we have been a part;
- ❑ noting the questions that have been answered and the ones that remain.

PREPARE
- ❑ Place water and drinking glasses on a side table that is easily accessible to all.
- ❑ Place a loaf of bread on the table; this will be used in the closing time.
- ❑ Post the "Welcome" page for people to see as they arrive.
- ❑ Place a candle on a central table; have matches ready.

❑ Have extra copies of the paraphrase of "The Prayer of Jesus," available (page 45).

❑ Write these three sentence stems on newsprint for use during "Connect":

- When I came to this program, I had these questions and uncertainties about my life of faith:…

- As I leave, I recognize that I have these new convictions and passions:…

- And these are the questions and wonderings I will carry for further exploration:…

WELCOME

Make sure the following words of welcome and instruction are written on newsprint and displayed in a spot where everyone can read them as they arrive:

Welcome to Session 12, In the End: A New Beginning
As you wait for the session to begin, sit with another group member and reflect on the highlights in the life of this learning community, of which you have been an important member.

OPEN

I welcome you for the last time to this community of exploration and learning.

There has been a place here for you. Your presence has made a difference to every one of these people who have accompanied you and who have been accompanied by you.

There has been a light here in the flame of this candle. (Light the candle.)

We have known again the truth that the light came into the darkness and the darkness has not put it out.

There has been water for refreshment. (Indicate the presence of water and glasses.)

We have known again the truth that living water flows abundantly for all and is here to be shared.

There has been a company of searchers who went with you on this journey of rediscovery.

We have known again the truth that a community of learners includes people who know both fear and love, and who seek to live with courage and passion.

Perhaps you recall a metaphor from our first session together, the one that Marcus Borg quotes from Kenneth Burke. Hear it again.

"Imagine that you enter a parlor. You come late. When you arrive, others have long preceded you, and they are engaged in a heated discussion, a discussion too heated for them to pause and tell you exactly what it is about. In fact, the discussion had already begun long before any of them got there, so that no one present is qualified to retrace for you all the steps that had gone before. You listen for a while; then you put in your oar. Someone answers; you answer him; another comes to your defense; another aligns herself against you, to either the embarrassment or gratification of your opponent, depending upon the quality of your ally's assistance. However the discussion is interminable. The hour grows late, you must depart. And you do depart, with the discussion still vigorously in progress."

As we began the course, we noted that our task was to continue to participate in the "Unending Conversation" of Christian theology. Now the hour grows late and we must depart. The discussion is still vigorously in progress, but this part of it is over. We will all go on and rejoin the conversation in another time and place. It's important that we leave this particular experience of the unending conversation behind and move on.

Let's begin our process of moving on, evaluating, and celebrating...

CONNECT

First, take 15 minutes to complete these three stem statements:

- When I came to this program, I had these questions and uncertainties about my life of faith:...
- As I leave, I recognize that I have these new convictions and passions:...
- And these are the questions and wonderings I will carry for further exploration:...

Find two other people and share with one another your responses to these sentence stems.

ENGAGE

Engage: Program Evaluation in Small Groups

Staying in small groups, respond together to these sentence stems. Have one person keep notes, which will be handed in to the facilitator.

- When repeating the program, be sure to do this again...
- And consider changing this...

There may be some benefit in discussing in the total group the responses to these general program evaluation questions. See if people need more time to complete their written program evaluations. When they are finished, collect them.

ANTICIPATE

Another important conversation at the end of this experience addresses the influence of this program on this congregation, or the congregation of which you are a part. Staying in small groups talk about these two things:

- new ways for me to think about my role, responsibilities, and opportunities in my community of faith;
- what we've experienced that influences what we do as an ongoing community of faith.

CLOSE

Engaging in a 12-session process of learning together generates a lot of group "history" and a new awareness of those who journeyed with you. Look around the group now and see again the people you have accompanied and who have accompanied you:

- a person who has a way of speaking directly and honestly and not beating around the bush,
- a person who brings energy to a group through their positive attitude,
- a person who struggles courageously with the reality of constant change in life,
- a person who asks the questions that others couldn't quite find words for,
- a person who ensures that others' needs are attended to, as well as their own,
- a person who lives their faith from a grounded faith and spirituality,
- a person who knows a lot and who is humbly open to learning more,
- a person who is angry at abuse and injustice and who takes public action to stop it,
- a person whose disability does not prevent them from being fully a member of the group.

Thinking of the members of the group in this way can enable you to be conscious of the variety of gifts individuals have brought to the life of this learning community. Take a moment *in silence* to think of the members of the group in this way.

Litany of Thanksgiving

As we continue in this time of thanksgiving, I invite all of you to name things related to the course for which you feel gratitude.

After each statement of thanksgiving, everyone will respond, "Holy One, we give you thanks."

Scripture

In our first session together, we offered one another bread and spoke a blessing: "Bread for the Journey." At that time, we were embarking on this journey of faithful learning. Now we move on from this experience to the next adventure and, as we do so, we offer blessings once again with the bread.

As they came near the village to which they were going, he walked ahead as if he were going on. But they urged him strongly, saying, "Stay with us, because it is almost evening and the day is now nearly over." So he went in to stay with them.

When he was at the table with them, he took bread, blessed and broke it, and gave it to them. Then their eyes were opened, and they recognized him; and he vanished from their sight.

They said to each other, "Were not our hearts burning within us while he was talking to us on the road, while he was opening the scriptures to us?"

That same hour they got up and returned to Jerusalem; and they found the eleven and their companions gathered together. They were saying, "The Lord has risen indeed, and he has appeared to Simon!" Then they told what had happened on the road, and how he had been made known to them in the breaking of the bread.

– Luke 24:28–35

As we offer bread to one another we will say, "Bread for the Journey."

Share the bread with each other.

As we come to the end of this time of learning in community, we will say again, as has been our practice, the paraphrase of the Prayer of Jesus. Let us pray together.

David Szabo Photography, Penticton, BC

For 24 years, TIM SCORER was a member of the Management Team at Naramata Centre, a retreat and education center of the United Church of Canada, where he worked in the areas of program planning and development, human interaction, leadership development, and spiritual formation. Tim has now joined the Ministry Leadership Team at Penticton United Church. There, he has particular responsibility for small group ministry, leadership development, faith formation, and spiritual direction. He is the father of three and grandfather of two and lives with his wife, Donna, in Naramata, British Columbia.

This program guide assumes that each participant will have purchased their own copy of *The Heart of Christianity* by Marcus Borg.

The Heart of Christianity:Rediscovering a Life of Faith
(San Francisco: HarperSanFrancisco, 2003, 2004)

Hard cover: ISBN 0-06-052676-9
CDN $34.95/USA $22.95

Soft cover: ISBN 0-06--73-684
CDN $20.95/USA $14.95